FOCUS ON COMPOSITION

FOCUS
ON COMPOSITION

ANN RAIMES

OXFORD UNIVERSITY PRESS

Oxford University Press

200 Madison Avenue,
New York, N.Y. 10016 USA

Walton Street,
Oxford OX2 6DP England

OXFORD is a trademark of Oxford University Press.

Library of Congress Cataloging in Publication Data
Raimes, Ann 1938-
Focus on composition.
Includes index.
1. English language—Composition and exercises.
2. English language—Text-books for foreigners.
3. English language—Grammar—1950-   I. Title.
PE1408.R15   428'.2   77-12969
ISBN 0-19-502238-6

Printing (last digit): 20 19 18 17 16

Cover design by Egon Lauterberg

Printed in Hong Kong

To my 3 R's:

        J. R.

        E. R.

        L. R.

PREFACE

Composition textbooks vary considerably, as do composition classes. Some require students to learn the grammatical forms of standard edited English by means of sentence drills or controlled compositions; some require students to imitate rhetorical models; some advocate pages and pages of "free" writing. It is the complexity of the composing process which accounts for the plethora of textbooks, each of which usually emphasizes one aspect of the process. And of course there have been long and heated disputes about what should be emphasized: whether a teacher should stress quantity in student writing or quality, fluency or accuracy, free or controlled writing, rhetoric or syntax. Teachers have tried just about everything.

But while teachers may disagree on methods and materials, most do agree that finding something to say, organizing it, and saying it well are what composition is all about. The Aristotelian division of classical rhetoric into Invention, Arrangement, and Style is in fact still valid today. The debate is over how much emphasis should be given to which elements of the complex process, and when.

It is precisely its complexity that makes composition both a challenge and a joy. And it need not be difficult. If it seems difficult, this text should help.

The problem for a composition teacher at the beginning of a term is not only that all students in the class may be at different levels or vary in their abilities. In addition, each individual student may have some sophisticated rhetorical skills and at the same time some glaring syntactic weaknesses— or the other way around. The teacher's problem, then, is to increase both types of skill within each student. This book provides a feasible way of working on both these skills at the same time.

Focus On Composition acknowledges the importance of both syntax[1] and rhetoric in composition, but recognizes too that they do not necessarily form a neat pedagogical sequence. Students do not have to master the

---

1. I use the terms **syntax** and **syntactic** throughout this book to include inflections, word choice, and sentence structure.

syntax of the "mature" sentence before they can deal with the rhetorical organization of ideas.

Each chapter in this book begins by presenting the student with a work of art, literature, popular culture, journalism, or science to respond to in writing. This is "free" writing inasmuch as the student expresses his[2] own ideas on the topic. He invents and organizes his own responses. But there is control here too. The topic, by its very nature, exercises it. It leads the student to choose particular modes of discourse, whether description, narration, exposition, or argument, and particular methods of development, such as chronological order, definition, or comparison and contrast. At the same time it also leads the student to the natural use of particular syntactic structures.

For example, if a writer is describing a static scene, he must make choices about how he will organize his description: will it be in spatial, climactic, or random order? And in describing the scene, he will almost inevitably be forced to use **there is** or **there are,** prepositions of place, and the present tense. The result: the teacher has a rhetorical and a syntactic focus for correcting the "free" composition and for directing the student to further assignments. If, for instance, the student clearly has difficulty in making verbs agree with subjects, he can be referred immediately to syntactic tasks that focus on that problem. This is the place for controlled compositions (which, in reality, have much to do with control but little to do with composition). If, on the other hand, the student has clearly mastered the relevant syntactic structures, he can move on to exercises that let him make more choices about organizing his own ideas. These composition exercises give him essential practice with the rhetorical structure of standard edited written English, which is different from the structure of spoken English and from the rhetorical structure of other languages.

Students using this text write in response to intellectually challenging topics; they grapple with complex ideas; generate their own sentences, paragraphs, and essays; read and react to each other's compositions; ask questions about their own and each other's writing; work on tasks appropriate to their own level; move at their own pace, according to their own skills, within each chapter; practice using syntactic structures and then have the opportunity to transfer the concepts into their own free writing. There is provision for class discussion, small-group work, individual work, in-class and at-home writing. The text concentrates on composition tasks and avoids lengthy explanations and examples of rhetorical methods. It devotes little time and space to grammatical terminology and detailed explanations of sentence structure. It concentrates on the many options

---

2. In this preface and throughout the book, I have used the masculine pronoun form to refer to teachers, students, writers, and readers. I feel that the **s/he, her/him, her/his** forms are not only distracting and tedious, but that they might also result in confusion for the students. There are times when grace and convention have to win out over conviction.

open to the writer and refrains from demanding any one correct answer. When students use this text, **they** compose and they work on their own compositions.

ACKNOWLEDGMENTS

Thanks go to many for their contributions to this book. Throughout years of teaching, discussions with colleagues produced such a quantity of good and exciting ideas, passed on from teacher to teacher, that it was sometimes easy to lose sight of where an idea originated. Grateful acknowledgments are therefore due to all those who have inspired ideas for this book. In particular, colleagues Linda Ann Kunz, Lou Inturrisi, Merry Sabet, and Hortense Sarot read parts of the manuscript and offered materials, suggestions, and support. David Davidson and James Kohn provided a great deal of useful criticism. I am indebted to Robert Allen of Teachers College, Columbia University and to Linda Ann Kunz of Hunter College for the technique derived from Sector Analysis and X-Word grammar of using a **yes/no** question to test sentence boundaries. My editor at Oxford University Press, Marilyn Rosenthal, worked on the manuscript with wisdom and unfailing good humor. Friends Roberta Bernstein and Deborah Nevins were always there to help. Essential contributions were made by my students in the Developmental English Program at Hunter College, who worked with the materials and did not hesitate to let me know—in their reactions and in their written results—when a task was not appropriate, and most of all by my husband, James Raimes, who read, commented, advised and, while I was writing, cooked, played with the children, took them out, put them to bed—and never complained.

New York City   A. R.
July 1977

CONTENTS

TO THE TEACHER:
HOW TO USE THIS BOOK

Focus on Composition is designed for:
— intermediate-advanced learners of English as a second language at the high school or college level,
— native speakers of English at the high school or college level who are "basic writing students."[1]

The text contains enough material for a one or two semester course, depending on the number of class hours per week and on the number of tasks assigned to each student.

Syntactic tasks are presented as they relate to the composition topics; they are not presented in order of difficulty, nor in a linguistically sequential order. As this text is not a survey of the structure of English, explanations and terminology have been kept to a minimum so the teacher can in addition assign a handbook, a grammar reference text or drill exercises.

CLASSROOM PROCEDURES

The following procedures are recommended. More detailed suggestions follow in the section "Working Through a Chapter" on p. xv.

1. The students work together in class on each task in the Core Composition section. Each student writes a composition.
2. The teacher corrects the composition, dealing specifically with those rhetorical and syntactic structures covered in the chapter.
3. The teacher then uses the errors, efforts, and problems revealed in the composition to determine each student's needs and to assign the appropriate syntactic tasks (Focus A) and/or rhetorical tasks (Focus B). From this point on, students can work individually or in small groups, in class or at home.
4. The whole class comes together again to work on the next Core Composition.

1. I am using the term "basic writing students" in the sense that Mina P. Shaughnessy does in **Errors and Expectations** (New York: Oxford University Press, 1977). She considers basic writing students as those who "write the way they do, not because they are slow or non-verbal, indifferent to or incapable of academic excellence, but because they are beginners and must, like all beginners, learn by making mistakes." (p. 5)

The composition topics begin with description and progress through narration and explanation to argument. If students work through the chapters in sequence, they will be able to apply principles learned in description to the more complex mode of argument. However, the material in the chapters does not increase in difficulty—there are challenging tasks in every chapter—so chapters and tasks can be used out of sequence.

THE ORGANIZATION OF THE BOOK

The book consists of the following parts:

Comprehensive Chapter Guide

The Comprehensive Chapter Guide lists all the syntactic and rhetorical structures covered in the tasks and all the source material used. The teacher can use this as a handy reference to assign specific tasks to students. Two special features have been included:

— one dot (•) next to the Task number in Focus A indicates a task of average difficulty; two dots (• •) indicate a more challenging task.
— the symbol (§) followed by a number indicates that the syntactic task is related to that preceding task, which should also be assigned.

The Chapters

The fourteen chapters are devoted to rhetorical modes and methods of development and to the syntactic structures generated by them. Each chapter contains a title page; a brief Introduction; a Core Composition related to a work of art, literature, popular culture, or scientific writing; tasks in which students practice using specific syntactic structures; a discussion of rhetorical structure; and composition tasks that direct students to various methods of development and organization of essays.

The next section on "Working Through a Chapter" will describe a chapter and detail procedures for working through it.

The Appendix

The Appendix contains the complete versions of reading passages used in completion exercises. Students who have worked on the syntactic structure of a passage, filling in blanks or combining sentences, will thus have the opportunity to see the passage as a whole piece of writing. It should be stressed that in many cases the wording of the original is not the only possible choice. The student's choice might be just as acceptable.

The Syntactic Index

A teacher who does not expect to use every chapter in the book can easily find and assign syntactic tasks from any chapter by means of this index.

WORKING THROUGH A CHAPTER

The Title Page

Both teachers and students will find the title page useful. When marking a composition, teachers can focus specifically on those structures in the composition which are dealt with in the chapter. They can thus limit their remarks and not overwhelm a student with red-ink corrections. They can use the list of structures on the title page to refer students to preview or review explanations or exercises in any other assigned handbooks or reference texts. The students will know what they are responsible for in their compositions in the chapter; they will know what they have to concentrate on as they edit, write drafts, and revise.

The Introduction

The Introduction discusses very briefly the type of writing that will be done in the chapter. It relates the topic of each chapter to speech and to real-life situations. This can be read by every student before the class begins to work on the Core Composition, or it can be read aloud by the teacher and discussed by the students. The students can then add their own ideas about the occasions when activities that are familiar in speech, such as comparing and contrasting or arguing, are appropriate in writing.

The Core Composition

The Core Composition is a writing assignment based on the stimulus of a picture or an interesting reading passage. Each Core Composition section includes questions to stimulate discussion about the student's composition.

The whole class works at the same time on each task in order. The text gives an explicit sequence of group and individual activities for the Core Composition, but these can be easily adapted to whole-class activities. To introduce the picture or the reading at the appropriate point, for example, the teacher could ask one student to describe the picture or passage to the whole class; or the teacher could read the passage aloud to the students, who would then summarize it; or the whole class could discuss the picture or passage before any writing is done.

In this and other parts of the chapter, words in the reading passages that might cause difficulty are marked with an asterisk (*) and glossed. They are glossed in the form in which they occur.

The directions for the Core Composition suggest that students work in pairs or groups. (For suggestions for group techniques, see "Using Small Groups in the Classroom," on p. xx.) Generally, this group activity is suggested as a technique to aid in pre-writing, editing, or revising, while the actual writing of the Core Composition is done alone by each individual student. If class time is short, the writing of the composition can be done as a home assignment, as long as the students read, ask questions about, and discuss their own and other students' compositions in the following class session. Writers need readers, and student writers need student readers.

A feature of each Core Composition section is a list of **Questions** for the writer to ask about his own composition and/or about other students' compositions. If a whole-class approach is preferred, the teacher can address these questions to individual students in the class or to the class as a whole. In most chapters, students are asked to write their answers to the questions. Their answers can be read to the group or class, handed in to the teacher along with the composition, or just kept by the students to attach to their returned compositions to help them revise or rewrite. Many of the questions are challenging and students are not expected to discover a "right answer" each time. The questions are designed to gradually develop an awareness of the writing process and the habit of critical questioning. If this critical questioning provokes some students to want to revise and rewrite their Core Composition (and in the author's experience, they often do), then students should be given additional time for this very valuable part of the writing process.

Correcting the Core Composition and Giving Assignments

A suggested procedure for correcting the composition is:

1. Use the title page of the chapter to determine what you will look for.
2. At the end of the composition, write comments, questions, and suggestions for improving the rhetorical organization.
3. Underline errors in the syntactic structures in focus and note the type of error in the margin if the student is familiar with grammatical terminology. A sample corrected composition is included, below.
4. Either ignore any other syntactic errors or write the correct form in the student's composition.
5. From this point on, each student's assignments in the chapter can be individualized. If a student makes an error with any of the syntactic structures that are the focus of the chapter, assign the appropriate tasks in Focus A.

The Comprehensive Chapter Guide lists the structures that the student will practice and indicates the level of difficulty of each task. If many students in the class show they have difficulties with the same syntactic structures, then the whole class can be directed to work on the same tasks. Assign Focus B tasks to students who need more practice in rhetorical organization.

A Sample Corrected Composition

MAGRITTE'S PORTRAIT

The biggest object that is represented <u>on</u> this	*preposition*
painting is a glass bottle. The bottle is <u>fell</u> with	*filled*
dark liquid. There is <u>a</u> empty transparent glass in	*article*
front of <u>the</u> plate. The plate has a slice of ham with	*Which plate?*
an eye in it. There <u>are</u> <u>a</u> silverware<u>s</u> that <u>are</u> a	*agreement—*
knife and fork. Both of them are placed on the	*uncountable*
rig<u>th</u> side of the plate.	*spelling*

You mention the eye very casually, right in the middle of your description, as if it appears on a table as often as a knife and fork. Can you change the order of your description so that the reader will really notice the eye? I think the reader would also like to know what "this painting" is.

Now work on Focus A, Tasks, 4, 6, 7, 8, 11, 12, and Focus B, Task 6.

Focus A: Syntactic Structure

Focus A tasks are short; they can be written and quickly corrected in class. They are not sequenced according to difficulty; a student will not get a progressive review of syntax by working through the Focus A tasks one by one. No student is expected to do all the tasks: some may do five or six, while others may do none. (The more syntactically accurate a student's writing is, the fewer syntactic tasks he will be assigned.) The more challenging tasks, indicated by two dots, are for assignment to the more proficient students.

Tasks either refer back to the subject matter of the Core Composition or stand alone; only a few are linked sequentially and these are marked with (§) in the text and the Comprehensive Chapter Guide.

Tasks are designated as group tasks, individual tasks, or group or individual tasks. "Using Small Groups in the Classroom," on p. xx, gives suggestions for assigning tasks as group activities.

Tasks include the following types:

a. Controlled compositions: the student rewrites a passage, making specific changes, such as changing present tense to past tense, or singular to plural.

b. Guided compositions: the student writes a paragraph or a series of paragraphs on a given topic following specific instructions (such as "use the
past tense") or using suggested structure vocabulary.

c. The student reads a passage with words omitted and fills in the blanks (a
cloze-type passage). Complete versions of all passages excerpted in this
way are included in the Appendix. Difficult words in the reading passages
are marked with an asterisk and glossed.

d. Sentence-completion or sentence-production exercises.

e. Sentence combining: the student explores stylistic options by embed-
ding one sentence in another. Many of the base sentences are derived
from passages used in the text, so students (individually or in groups) can
try to discover all the available options, choose the one they prefer, and
then check to see which one the professional writer used.

f. Writing sentences as **yes/no** questions. The **yes/no** question writing is a
technique to test for sentence division, to find out where sentences begin
and end. The teacher should stress, therefore, that the questions produced will not necessarily be used in speech or writing: the purpose of
the question-making is to find and edit fragments and run-ons. Students
look for the subject and predicate of the main clause, make a question
from them and attach all other sentence parts to that question. The only
words they can add are **do, does,** or **did,** which are followed by the base
form of the verb. Examples are:

The boy sitting on the fence is her brother.
Is the boy sitting on the fence her brother?

Yesterday evening they all went to the movies.
Did they all go to the movies yesterday evening?

But if a student applies the same test to:

The boy sitting on the fence he is her brother.

he will usually find the redundant **he.** Similarly, if a student writes a fragment like:

Because it was raining hard all day.

the **yes/no** question test gives him a concrete method of finding out if it is
a sentence or a fragment. It has a subject and a predicate, but what does
he do with that **because**? He can either drop it:

It was raining hard all day.

or attach this sentence part to another base sentence:

Because it was raining hard all day, I stayed home.

   If a student writes run-on sentences, the **yes/no** question test will tell
him that if he makes two questions, he must make two sentences. The

only words he can use with a comma to join two sentences are **and, but, or, nor, so, for,** and **yet.** Look at the run-on sentence:

It is raining I am staying home.

There are two questions here:

Is it raining? Am I staying home?

So there should be two sentences, and the student has the following options:

a. to use a period:

It is raining. I am staying home.

b. to use a semi-colon:

It is raining; I am staying home.

c. to use a coordinator:

It is raining, so I am staying home.

d. to subordinate:

Because it is raining, I am staying home.

Many students have difficulty with determining sentence boundaries in writing. Tasks 1 and 2 in Focus A Chapter 1, and Task 7 in Focus A Chapter 3, introduce the **yes/no** question test with an explanation and exercises. It is recommended that these tasks be assigned to **all** students at the beginning of the course, so that they can then apply the technique in their editing of each composition assignment.

After a student has completed the assigned syntactic tasks, he can then be directed to go back to his original Core Composition to correct the errors the teacher indicated. Or he can move on to a Focus B task.

ocus B: Rhetorical Structure

All students should read the discussion of the rhetorical structure at the beginning of each Focus B section and should be encouraged to continue the technique, introduced with the Core Composition, of asking questions about their own writing. All students should be assigned at least one Focus B task in each chapter. Students who are assigned very few syntactic tasks might work on two or even three compositions, concentrating on invention and organization of ideas. Some library assignments are included in Focus B for students in an academic setting, and teachers will probably need to recommend basic source materials, put books on reserve, or refer students to the services of a reference librarian. Students can work on Focus B tasks in the library, at home, or in class. Two students working on the same task should be encouraged to read and comment on each other's work.

USING SMALL GROUPS IN THE CLASSROOM

The directions for Core Composition tasks recommend that students work together to discuss, plan, and edit their writing. Many of the Focus A tasks are designated as group tasks as well. Small groups provide an opportunity for students to work on their own problems; peer response and peer instruction is encouraged, and the classroom becomes student-centered instead of teacher-centered.

When a class is divided into three to five activity groups, the teacher can move from group to group asking questions, giving advice, and helping with directions and explanations. Often just a finger pointed at a wrong verb form is enough to make a student aware of the error. Roles can also be assigned to members of the group: discussion leader, note-taker, spelling checker, or proofreader, for example. A grouped classroom will be a noisier classroom than the traditional teacher-centered class, but students will constantly be involved in an activity and will be getting feedback both from their peers and their teacher. Their responsive audience will be increased—and that is an advantage for any writer.

If teachers feel that a whole-class approach is more suitable for their particular students, whole-class discussions can simply replace small-group discussions. For example, the instructions for the Core Composition of Chapter 1 ask for pairs of students to discuss what they see in Magritte's **Portrait.** A whole-class discussion could be substituted here, but the composition assignment—for each student to write a description —remains the same.

It is especially beneficial to students to work on syntactic tasks with other students. If a few students are assigned the same task, they can either do it individually and then compare results and produce one final version, or they can work through the task together until they agree and hand in one paper with all their names on it. Many of the tasks in Focus A are headed "group or individual task." These can be done by one student alone, or by a few students working together. Students working on a controlled composition, for example, discuss the changes they would make, decide on the best choice when there are alternatives, and produce one final version. To do that, they will very often get involved in heated discussions about where to put a comma or which verb tense to use. With Focus A tasks, the classroom can become an open workshop, with groups and individual students working on their own specific writing problems.

Tasks used as group tasks become teaching instead of testing tasks, and —even more of an advantage—it is the students who teach each other. The teacher and this book will help them do that.

COMPREHENSIVE CHAPTER GUIDE

- average-level task
- • challenging task
- (§) task is linked to the task number inside the parentheses

FOCUS ON COMPOSITION

1

DESCRIBING A STATIC SCENE

Focus on these syntactic structures

        sentence division and punctuation
                subject and predicate
                fragments and run-ons
                yes/no questions
        prepositions of place
        agreement: **there is** and **there are**
        countable and uncountable nouns
        determiners
                articles (**a, an, the**)
                quantity words (**some, much, many,** etc.)
        -s inflection
        sentence combining

Focus on these rhetorical structures

        organizing a paragraph
                spatial order
                climactic order
        giving a full, accurate picture

INTRODUCTION

In this chapter, you will focus on writing descriptions. You will have to observe carefully, with all of your senses. Your reader should be able to make his own accurate picture from your description. In speech, you often describe static (not moving) scenes: you tell a friend about the mess in a room after a party, or you describe a bus station waiting room where you spent a few miserable hours. When you **write** description, you have to give even more details as you don't have your face, voice, or gestures to help you. Try describing a spiral staircase without using your hands or body movements—you have to rely totally on your words.

CORE COMPOSITION

1. Look closely at Magritte's **Portrait** and examine each object in turn. With a partner, discuss what you see in the picture.

2. Magritte presents his image with a brush and oil paints. Can you, with a pen and words, present as clear an image to your reader as Magritte presents to the viewer of his picture? Individually, write a short paragraph describing the picture as accurately and as fully as you can. Repaint the picture with words, as if you were describing it for a blind person to "see." Do not try to interpret or explain why Magritte painted the picture or what the picture means. Just describe what the picture shows.

3. Write your answers to the questions below.

Questions What did you mention first?

What did you mention last?

Why did you choose to do it that way?

Where in your paragraph did you mention the eye?

How would your paragraph change if you moved sentences around in it? Try it.

What is the most striking part of the painting?

Where is it in the painting?

Where did you mention it in your paragraph?

How many sentences did you write?

4. Read your partner's paragraph. Discuss with your partner how each of you answered the questions.

5. If you have discovered a more effective way to organize your paragraph, rewrite it.

4

René Magritte, **Portrait** (1935). Oil on canvas, 28⅞" × 19⅞". Collection, The Museum of Modern Art, New York. Gift of Kay Sage Tanguy.

FOCUS A: SYNTACTIC STRUCTURE

Do the tasks your teacher recommends.

• 1. Task (group or individual)

Look at the divisions in the sentences below:

Subject	Predicate
The meal	<u>is</u> ready.
The bottle	<u>is</u> full.
Someone	<u>has drunk</u> a glass of wine.
A slice of ham.	<u>is lying</u> on the plate.
The ham	<u>looks</u> delicious.
The ham lying on the plate	<u>looks</u> delicious.
The artist	<u>is</u> probably <u>going to eat</u> the ham.

The sentences have been divided into subject and predicate. The predicate contains the verb phrase of the sentence. Each verb phrase of the predicate is underlined. Divide the following sentences into subject and predicate and underline the verb phrase in each:

a. Gary Cooper is a movie star.
b. Gary Cooper can ride well.
c. The cowboy is riding a black horse.
d. Horses are loyal animals.
e. Cowboys own their own horses.
f. The man from the far West rode over the mountains.
g. He has been thinking about revenge.
h. A shot was heard all over the valley.

• • 2. Task (group or individual)

A base sentence (subject + predicate) can always be made into a question that you can answer with **yes** or **no**.

Examples The meal is ready.
Is the meal ready?

Someone has drunk a glass of wine.
Has someone drunk a glass of wine?

A slice of ham is lying on the plate.
Is a slice of ham lying on the plate?

You do not need to leave out, change, or add words. All you need to do is move the auxiliary verb (the first or only word of the verb phrase). These auxiliary verbs are: **am, is, are, was, were, has, have, had, will, would, shall,**

should, can, could, may, might, must. Sometimes you will have to add **do, does,** or **did** to make a question.

Examples The ham looks delicious.
Does the ham look delicious? (**looks = does look**)
The pears look delicious.
Do the pears look delicious? (**look = do look**)
The ham looked delicious.
Did the ham look delicious? (**looked = did look**)

You can use this **yes/no** question test to check where sentences begin and end. **A complete base sentence will always turn into a yes/no question.** If you have to add any word other than **do, does** or **did,** or if you have to leave out any words, then the "sentence" is not a sentence. It might be a fragment:

If you feel hungry.
A glass standing on the table.
The ham which is lying on the plate.

If you try to turn these into **yes/no** questions, using all the words there, and only the words there, you cannot do it.
Or it might be two sentences run together (a run-on):

The bottle is on the table it is full of wine.
There is a glass on the table, however, it is empty.

If you try to turn these into **yes/no** questions, you will make two questions for each (Is the bottle on the table? Is it full of wine?)

If you find fragments or run-ons by using the **yes/no** question test, then you can correct them.

Here are two examples of how you could make the fragment **If you feel hungry** into a complete sentence:

Fragment   **Sentence**
If you feel hungry.   You feel hungry.
                      If you feel hungry, you should eat something.

Here are three ways to correct the run-on sentence:
The bottle is on the table it is full of wine.

1. Divide into two sentences by using a period (.) and a capital letter.
The bottle is on the table. It is full of wine.

2. Separate with a semicolon (;).
The bottle is on the table; it is full of wine.

3. Join with a comma (,) and one of the following words: **and, but, or, nor, so, for, yet.**
The bottle is on the table, and it is full of wine.

Write **S** next to all complete and correctly punctuated sentences in the examples that follow. Write **F** or **R** next to fragments or run-ons. Rewrite any fragments or run-ons as complete, separated sentences.

a. Carpentry is useful.

b. Is fun, too.

c. You get a very satisfied feeling.

d. When you work with wood and make something.

e. You need a few basic tools, they are not very expensive.

f. A hammer, a saw, a measuring tape, a square, nails, screws, and glue.

g. An electric drill is useful, but you can manage without it.

h. An electric saw is useful you can manage without it.

i. Patience is something that a good carpenter must have.

j. Because it is essential to measure and cut accurately.

k. If you don't, your piece of furniture might be crooked.

l. Like my first piece was.

• 3. Task (group or individual)

Add capital letters and punctuation to the following passage:

more so than at other meals there is a wide difference in the tastes of breakfast eaters some people teenage girls especially prefer to eat no breakfast at all or perhaps a piece of toast and a glass of milk many women take only a cup of coffee and a glass of juice while others eat a hearty morning meal and watch their calories at lunchtime men generally like a more substantial meal sometimes two or three courses including fruit cereal and eggs unlike other meals breakfast may and should be prepared to order

Now underline all the verb phrases in the passage. (The complete version, from Emily Post's **Etiquette,** is on page 11.

• 4. Task (individual)

Write an accurate description of a table set for a meal at your home or in a restaurant. Describe the objects and their position on the table, so that your reader will be able to picture clearly what you actually see.

Vocabulary hints on the right/left; to the right of/left of; in the corner (of a room); on the corner (of a table, a street); at the top; at the bottom; in the mid-

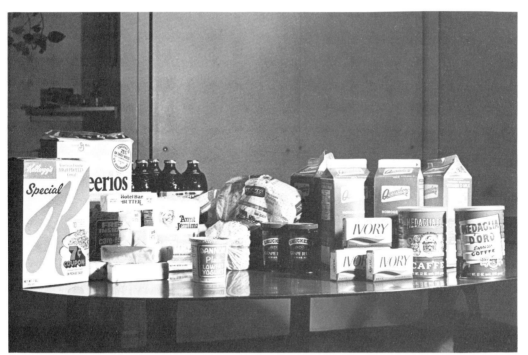

Sara Cedar Miller, **Objects on Table.** Courtesy of Sara Cedar Miller.

dle; above; below; beneath; behind; next to; adjacent to; parallel to; perpendicular to; vertical(ly); horizontal(ly); diagonal(ly); in the background/foreground

• 5. Task (group or individual)

Imagine that the picture by Magritte contained **two** of each of the items in the table setting: two plates, two forks, etc. Rewrite your description. Pay special attention to the use of **there is** or **there are.** If you are working with other students, discuss each change and make sure that you all agree on the form of the change.

• 6. Task (group or individual)

The photograph above shows part of a family's weekly groceries. Write twenty sentences telling about the things that the mother in this family buys regularly at the supermarket. Do not use exact numbers, like "three" or "five." Instead, use the general quantity words in the chart below. Match up the items with their containers. Follow the pattern of the example sentences.

Examples She buys **a few** cans of coffee.
She doesn't buy **many** cans of coffee.
She buys **a little** coffee.
She doesn't buy **much** coffee.

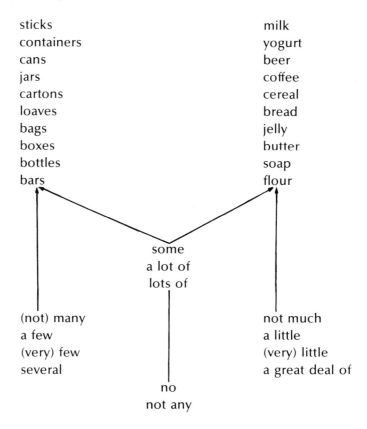

sticks   milk
containers   yogurt
cans   beer
jars   coffee
cartons   cereal
loaves   bread
bags   jelly
boxes   butter
bottles   soap
bars   flour

some
a lot of
lots of

(not) many   not much
a few   a little
(very) few   (very) little
several   a great deal of

no
not any

Now write six more sentences, using **no** and **not any**, and telling your reader about the items that the mother in the family does **not** buy.

Examples She doesn't buy **any** (cans of) fruit.
She buys **no** (cans of) fruit.

• 7. Task (group or individual)

Divide the words below into two lists:

A. Words that can follow **a** or **an** (countable)
B. Words that cannot follow **a** or **an** (uncountable)

ham   knife   food   furniture   butter   bread   milk   apple
orange   fruit   meat   wine   sandwich   money   hunger

happiness advice machine information news homework equipment poem poetry child man mankind anger

Write the plural forms of the words in your list A.
Write sentences using the words in your list B.

• 8. Task (group or individual)

Read the following passage:

BREAKFAST

More so than at other meals, there is a wide difference in the tastes of breakfast eaters. Some people, teenage girls especially, prefer to eat no breakfast at all—or perhaps a piece of toast and a glass of milk. Many women take only a cup of coffee and a glass of juice, while others eat a hearty* morning meal and watch their calories at lunchtime. Men generally like a more substantial* meal, some-times two or three courses, including fruit, cereal, and eggs. Unlike other meals, breakfast may, and should, be prepared "to order." That is, if daughter Susie truly dislikes eggs she may be given a dish of cold cereal, but Father should not therefore be deprived* of his scrambled eggs and bacon.

In setting the breakfast table, Mother puts out just those utensils which will be needed by each person.

A variety of cold cereals, milk, cream, sugar, salt and pepper, and jams or jellies may be placed in the center of the table or on a convenient side table, but whoever is doing the cooking serves the hot food directly onto the plates and places them in front of those sitting at the table. If your table is large enough a lazy Susan or turntable is most convenient and makes each item easily accessible* to everyone.

The setting is as follows:

Fork at the left of the plate.

Knife at the right of the plate.

Spoon for cereal at the right of the knife.

Teaspoon for fruit or grapefruit spoon at the right of the cereal spoon.

Butter knife across the bread-and-butter plate, which is to the left and above the fork.

Napkins, in rings or not, at the left of the plates.

Coffee cups with spoons lying at the right of the saucers or mugs, or at the right of each plate if the coffee is served from the kitchen. If it is served by Mother at the table, cups and saucers, mugs, and coffeepot are beside her place.

Glass for milk or water, to the right and above the spoons.

EMILY POST, **Etiquette**

*Gloss **hearty** big and nourishing
substantial large, solid
deprived of refused, denied
accessible to in reach of

In this passage, the items in the table setting are presented in the form of a list, in incomplete sentences. Make each sentence complete by adding articles (**a, an, the**) and verbs or verb phrases where necessary.

Example Change: **Fork at the left of the plate.** to: **Place the fork at the left of the plate.** or to: **The fork is put (placed) at the left of the plate.**

• 9. Task (group or individual)

From the passage about "Breakfast" in Task 8 make a list of all the words that have an added -s at the end. (If you remove the -s and still have a word, then that -s is an added -s.)

Compare eggs (= egg + added -s)
            glass

Now divide the words in your list into two groups:

with -s to show plural of noun

eggs

with -s to show 3rd. person singular of verb

serves

• 10. Task (group or individual)

Write sentences using the following words:

an egg	a book	a woman	a car
the egg	the book	the woman	the car
eggs	books	women	cars
the eggs	the books	the women	the cars

Examples Please give me **an apple.**
The apple you gave me was delicious.
Apples are good for you.
The apples I bought last week were very sweet.

• • 11. Task (group or individual)

Look at the diagram of the apartment in Chapter 14, p. 166. Imagine that you have just furnished it. Describe what furniture is in the apartment, and describe exactly where it is. Give details about the position of each item in the apartment and describe it fully: its size, color, design, and shape. Pay special attention to place words like: **in, on, under, behind, above, below, on top of, around, near, next to.** Pay attention also to your use of **there is** or **there are.**

Now exchange papers with another student. From his description, draw the apartment plan with the furniture in it. If the position of the furniture is not clear, check with the writer and ask him to clarify his description.

• 12. Task (group or individual)

Combine the groups of sentences below into **one** sentence only for each group. Keep the meaning the same. Some hints are given; try them all and choose the one you like the best.

Example There is a bottle on the table.
The bottle is full.

There is a full bottle on the table.
or: On the table there is a bottle, which is full.

HINTS
a _____ bottle |
which

a. You won't want to eat the ham.
The ham has an eye in it.

because | as | , so

b. There's a lot of wine.
You won't be able to drink it all.

, so | such a lot of wine that

c. Many women take only a cup of coffee.
Many women take only a glass of juice.

and | after

d. Some people eat a hearty morning meal.
They watch their calories at lunchtime.

and | after

e. Mother puts out just those utensils.
Those utensils will be needed by each person.

that | which

f. Mother sets the breakfast table.
She puts out the utensils.

when | -ing | whenever

FOCUS B: RHETORICAL STRUCTURE

Do the tasks your teacher recommends.

When you describe a scene, your reader should be able to "see" it clearly from your words. Your reader will see, hear, smell, feel, and taste only what you tell him. Accurate description is necessary for many people: for an architect describing a house plan; for a mechanic explaining where the carburetor is; for a technician describing laboratory apparatus; for a real estate agent describing an apartment; for a policeman describing the scene of a crime. When you describe, you have to make a lot of decisions: you have to decide which are the most important and the least important features of what you see, which details you will include and emphasize, what point you will describe the scene from, and in what order you will describe what you see. You might decide to describe a scene from left to right or from top to bottom (spatial order) or to organize details from the least important to the most important (climactic order). You also have to decide whether you will describe only what you see, or whether you will use your other senses too to describe what you hear, smell, feel, and taste. Remember that you are trying to give your reader an exact copy of your own experience. You are trying to let your reader experience through your words everything that you experienced. It is not enough to say, "There is a chair in the corner." Is it a hard chair or an upholstered chair? What is it made of? What color is it? What design is it? Is it comfortable? Is it old or new? Does it have any special features—a missing arm or a torn seat? If you don't give your reader a picture of the chair, he will form his own, and it could easily be very different from yours.

1. You have just been to an art gallery where you have seen Fantin-Latour's **Still Life.** Describe it to an art student who has never seen it but who needs to know exactly what is in the picture so that he can refer to it in an article he is writing. Give a full and accurate description of the painting.

2. Ask your teacher to set up an arrangement of pencils, books, Cuisenaire rods, Tinkertoys, furniture, or any other objects. Describe the arrangement in detail. Give another student your description and see if he can set up the same arrangement by using your description.

3. With other students, empty out the contents of a bag of objects, prepared by the teacher or by a student. Leave the objects in their random arrangement and describe them. What will you mention first? Last? What details will you include?

   Now try to redistribute the objects into groups according to size, shape, color, function, material, or any other criteria. Describe this new grouped arrangement. How many groups do you have? How many paragraphs will you have?

4. Describe the corner of the room photographed by Walker Evans (p. 16). Try to convey the main impression that the room makes. Describe each

Henri Fantin-Latour, **Still Life** (1810). Courtesy of the National Gallery of Art, Washington. Chester Dale Collection.

object in detail. Keep your description as objective as you can. Try not to react emotionally; just describe. Give your paragraph a title.

5. Describe the living area of the house of your dreams. Draw a floor plan first. Give a full description so that your reader can visualize the room exactly as it is in your mind.

   Describe the living area of the house of your dreams once again, but this time include only details that illustrate **one** important feature of the room, for example, its light, its space, its comfort, its color, or its simplicity. If you begin with "The living area of the house of my dreams is a blaze of color . . ." then what follows should describe the color in that room.

6. In an encyclopedia (to be found in the Reference Room of a library) look up the entry on "Still Life Painting." Find an encyclopedia that has a lot of illustrations; the 1970 edition of the **Encyclopaedia Brittanica,** for example, contains reproductions of many paintings. Choose one of the paintings reproduced and describe it in detail for a reader who has never seen it.

Walker Evans, **Interior, West Virginia Coal Miner's House** (July 1935). Photograph, $8\frac{15}{16}''$ × $7\frac{3}{16}''$. Collection, The Museum of Modern Art, New York.

2

DESCRIBING A PERSON

ocus on these syntactic structures

>determiners
>>quantity words (**some, much, many,** etc.) with countable
>>and uncountable nouns
>>articles (**a, an, the**)
>>possessives (**'s, s'**)
>pronouns: subject, object, possessive, reflexive
>sentence division and punctuation
>>subject and verb
>>**yes/no** questions
>agreement: singular/plural
>modifiers: adjectives and adverbs
>verbs
>>**be, do, have**
>>present tense
>>questions
>sentence combining

ocus on these rhetorical structures

>organizing a description
>>spatial order
>>climactic order
>emphasizing important features
>separating information and inference

INTRODUCTION

If you saw someone robbing a bank, you would have to give an accurate description of that person to the police. "He was quite tall and handsome, with dark hair, and he was wearing a green jacket" would not be as helpful as: "He was about 6'2"; he had dark curly hair, short and with no part; he had a long scar on his left cheek; he was wearing a dark green tweed jacket, gray pants, and black shoes."

If you had to tell someone how to find a friend of yours at a crowded station, you would give a full description of that friend, so that he could be found in a crowd. In everyday speech, you often describe a person: you tell your friends about someone unusual, or someone impressive, or someone you have just met (and maybe fallen in love with!). When you do that, you want your listener to be able to see the person the same way you do. In writing, too, it is important to include details and to emphasize important features.

CORE COMPOSITION

1. With other students, write down a list of single words to describe Gary Cooper as he appears in the picture from the movie **High Noon.** Compare your group's list with another group's.

   Which words describe the actual man? Which words express your personal judgment about him, based on his appearance? Divide your list of words into two lists.

Example	the man	my judgment
	tall	handsome
	walking	aggressive

Most people would trust their eyes and say that he is walking. Most people would also agree that he is tall; his height can be measured and compared to the height of other people. Not everyone, however, would agree that he is handsome, and there is no way of really knowing if his behavior is aggressive or not.

2. Discuss with other students what you would mention if you had to describe this man to someone who was looking for him. From his physical appearance, his clothes, his expression, and his posture, can you make any additional inferences (intelligent guesses) about his personality, his way of life, or his social and private life? What conclusions can you draw about him from this picture alone? Discuss these questions in your group. Then, individually, write about a page describing the man. Make at least three inferences about him. Refer to details in the picture to explain your inferences.

Gary Cooper in **High Noon** (1952). Courtesy of Ivy Film, New York. Photograph from The Museum of Modern Art, Film Stills Archive.

Vocabulary hints perhaps; possibly; it is probable/possible that; he is probably; he might; he may (be); maybe he

3. Individually, describe another student in your class or group. Describe in detail the physical appearance (face, hair, body, clothes) and then draw a few conclusions about the student's personality, experience, likes, dislikes, hobbies, ambitions, etc. Write two paragraphs.

4. Reread both of your compositions and write down your answers to the following questions. With another student, discuss and compare your answers to the questions.

Questions In your description of the man in **High Noon,** what physical feature did you mention first?

What did you mention last?

Were you trying to give an overall picture of the man, or were you emphasizing one important feature? Which one? Where did you mention it: at the beginning, middle, or end?

If you had to give your description a one-word title (such as "Determination"), what would your title be?

In your description of the student, what did you mention first? Why? What did you mention last? Why?

In either of your descriptions, did you describe the setting? Does the place help to describe the person's looks and character?

In either of your descriptions, did you make any comparisons, such as:

He **looks like** an avenger.
He **looks as if** he wants revenge.
He is **as** hard **as** nails.

Include some if you think they would make your description more accurate and specific.

FOCUS A: SYNTACTIC STRUCTURE

Do the tasks your teacher recommends.

• 1. Task (group or individual)

Which of the following words are used with **much** and which with **many**? Make two lists.

friends effort furniture luggage time times occasions
advice ideas information food eggs employment people
happiness business pleasure news

• • 2. Task (group or individual)

Try to imagine what kind of person a typical cowboy is: the way he lives, his likes and dislikes, his possessions. Write sentences telling what he has, owns, needs, likes, shows, endures, and wants. Use words listed below and with them use the quantity words in the chart in Task 6, p. 10. Write fifteen sentences in all, selecting words from both the **countable** and the **uncountable** nouns below. Use the present tense.

countable	uncountable
books	sleep
showers	furniture
guns	peace
bullets	fresh air
boots	sunshine
horses	food
hats	patience

20

friends	courage
saddles	honor
wounds	money
scars	pain
enemies	loneliness

Examples He doesn't take **many** showers.
He has **a lot of** guns.
He has **a great deal of** courage.

• **3.** Task (group or individual)

Underline the correct pronoun form in the sentences below. Use the chart to help you.

SUBJECT	OBJECT	POSSESSIVE		REFLEXIVE
I	me	my	mine	myself
we	us	our	ours	ourselves
you	you	your	yours	yourself
				yourselves
he	him	his	his	himself
she	her	her	hers	herself
it	it	its		itself
they	them	their	theirs	themselves

a. They invited (I/me) to the party.
b. I talked to (they/them) for hours.
c. Sally made a speech; Sam and (she/her) had just gotten engaged.
d. Jack and (I/me) decided to leave early.
e. They all said goodbye to Jack and (I/me).
f. We took an umbrella but soon realized that it wasn't (our/ours).
g. Sally said it was (her/hers).
h. The guests all enjoyed (them/theirs/themselves) immensely.

• • **4.** Task (group or individual)

Write one sentence about each of the topics listed below. In the sentence, use some pronouns from the chart in Task 3, above.

Topics a. a horse   b. violence   c. my family (we)   d. a doctor
e. students   f. society   g. an actress   h. educated people

Examples a cowboy: **He** puts on **his** hat before **he** looks at **himself** in the mirror.

cowboys: **They** carry guns to protect **themselves** and what is **theirs**.

• **5.** Task (group or individual)

Fill in the appropriate reflexive form of the pronoun.

Example People enjoy _____ at the opera.
People enjoy **themselves** at the opera.

Refer to the chart in Task 3, above, for the pronoun forms.

a. She was proud of _____ when she won the prize.
b. We promised _____ that we would take a break at the end of the day.
c. She looked at _____ in the mirror and smiled.
d. I don't want to deprive _____ of a good opportunity.
e. The cat washed _____ all over with its tongue.
f. Jack, you shouldn't tire _____ out by working too hard.
g. Children, you must get _____ ready for the trip.
h. The little boy dried _____ after his bath.

• • **6.** Task (group or individual)

Rewrite each one of the sentences below in two different ways, using possessive pronouns. See the chart in Task 3 in this chapter for pronoun forms.

Examples   That hat belongs to the actress.   That hat belongs to me.
     i. That is **her** hat.   i. That is **my** hat.
     ii. That hat is **hers**.   ii. That hat is **mine**.

a. That ranch belongs to the cowboy.
b. That ranch belongs to us.
c. That garter belongs to the dancer.
d. That saloon belongs to the twins.
e. This town belongs to the sheriff.
f. These guns belong to me.
g. Those horses belong to my brother and me.
h. This land belongs to the twins' mother.

• **7.** Task (group or individual)

Underline the verb phrase in each sentence in Task 6, above. Circle the subject of each sentence. Rewrite each sentence as a question that can be answered with **yes** or **no** (a **yes/no** question).

Example (That hat) belongs to the actress.
Does that hat belong to the actress?

• 8. Task (individual)

Imagine that the picture of Gary Cooper on p. 19 shows twin cowboys walking along together. Rewrite the paragraph of description you wrote for the Core Composition of this chapter, changing **he** to **they.** Make all the other necessary changes, and underline each change you make.

• 9. Task (group or individual)

Add appropriate words in the blanks in the following passage.

Examples a, an, the (articles)
large, dirty, etc. (adjectives)

Doctor Parcival was a _____ man with _____ _____ mouth covered by _____ _____ mustache. He always wore a _____ _____ waistcoat out of the pockets of which pro-truded* _____ number of _____ kind of black cigars known as stogies. His teeth were _____ and _____ and there was something strange about his eyes. _____ lid of _____ left eye twitched; it fell down and snapped up; it was exactly as though the lid of _____ eye were _____ window shade and some-one stood inside _____ doctor's head playing with the cord.

SHERWOOD ANDERSON, **Winesburg, Ohio**

°**Gloss protruded** stuck out

(The original passage is in the Appendix on p. 168.)

• 10. Task (group or individual)

The verb phrases of the base sentences are in bold type in the passage from **Winesburg, Ohio** that appears on p. 168. Circle the subjects of the sentences.

• 11. Task (group or individual)

Write responses to the questions below, using the adverb form.

Example She is an aggressive person. How does she talk?
She talks aggressively.

Pay special attention to the last two (i and j). The adverb forms of **fast** and **hard** are irregular and do not take **-ly.**

a. She is a cautious driver. How does she drive?
b. She is a slow thinker. How does she think?

c. She is a fervent debater. How does she debate?
d. She is an extravagant spender. How does she spend?
e. She is an erratic tennis-player. How does she play tennis?
f. She is a skillful dancer. How does she dance?
g. She is a greedy eater. How does she eat?
h. She is an energetic runner. How does she run?
i. She is a fast walker. How does she walk?
j. She is a hard worker. How does she work?

• •12. Task (group or individual)

Examine carefully the details in Grant Wood's painting, **American Gothic.** Write a list of questions about the woman, asking who she is, what she does, and what she has. Then write another list of questions about the two people as a married couple, this time asking who they are, what they do, and what they have.

Examples Is she narrow-minded?
How many children does she have?
Does she wear jewelry?

Exchange your list of questions with another student. Write an answer to each question, using a complete sentence. Include words like **probably, possibly, perhaps, she might, it is possible that,** whenever you make an inference.

• • 13. Task (group or individual)

Write a list of words that could be used to describe the man in **American Gothic.** The words should fit into this sentence:

The man is _____. or The man looks _____.

Now write another list of words that describe what he is **not:**

The man is not _____.
The man does not look _____.

Compare your two lists. Which set of qualities would you prefer a relative to have? a friend? a politician? a teacher? a doctor? Why? What would you expect someone with your second set of qualities to look like and dress like? Discuss these questions and then write a short paragraph telling which set of qualities you would expect **one** of the people in the list above to have, and why.

Example I would like a politician to be serious and reliable. In addition he should be hard-working and honest. These qualities are necessary because . . .

24

Grant Wood, **American Gothic.** Courtesy of The Art Institute of Chicago.

• **14.** Task (group or individual)

How many people and how many bedrooms are being talked about in the
following sentences? For each sentence, answer **one** or **more than one.**

	How many people?	How many bedrooms?
a. Her daughter's bedroom is always untidy.		
b. Her daughters' bedroom is always untidy.		
c. Her daughters' bedrooms are always untidy.		
d. The child's bedroom is always untidy.		

25

How many   How many
people?   bedrooms?

e. The children's bedrooms are always untidy.
f. The children's bedroom is always untidy.
g. The boys' bedroom is always untidy.
h. Their son's bedroom is always untidy.
i. The parents' bedroom is incredibly neat.

• • 15. Task (individual)

Notice the use of the possessive apostrophe (') in these sentences:

The man's expression is serious. (singular) + 's
The boy's expression is serious. (singular) + 's
The men's expressions are serious. (plural, but no s) + 's
The boys' expressions are serious. (plural with s) + '

Write six sentences about the people in the painting **American Gothic** on p. 25 and about others in their family. Use possessives.

Examples The woman's education is very limited.
Their daughters' rooms are always neat.

• 16. Task (individual)

Write one sentence using each of the following words:

girl	school	waitress	child
girls	schools	waitresses	children
girl's	school's	waitress's	child's
girls'	schools'	waitresses'	children's

(§16) • • 17. Task (group)

Exchange with another student the sentences you wrote for Task 16. Substitute pronouns for all the above nouns in your partner's sentences.

Examples The boy is skating. He is skating.
The boys are laughing. They are laughing.
The boy's skate is loose. His skate is loose.
The boys' laughter rings out across the lake.
Their laughter rings out across the lake.

• 18. Task (group or individual)

Combine each group of sentences below into **one** sentence. Keep the meaning the same. Try all the hints given and choose the one you like best.

Examples Some people eat a hearty morning meal.
They watch their calories at lunchtime.

HINTS
and | and then | after |
after -ing

Some people eat a hearty morning meal and watch their calories at lunchtime.

Some people eat a hearty morning meal, and then they watch their calories at lunchtime.

Some people watch their calories at lunchtime after they have eaten a hearty morning meal.

Some people, after eating a hearty morning meal, watch their calories at lunchtime.

a. The woman looks stern.
The man looks stern.

and | both . . . and |
and so . . . | and . . . too

b. The cowboy is walking.
His walk is slow.
His walk is purposeful.

-'s | -ly | and

c. The cowboy has a star on his chest.
He has his hand on his gun.
He is the sheriff.

with | who |

d. The man is holding a pitchfork.
He is looking directly at his wife.

who | with | -ing

e. It is high noon.
There are no people on the street.

but | although

f. Doctor Parcival was a large man.
He had a drooping mouth.
His mouth was covered by a yellow mustache.

with | who | which

FOCUS B: RHETORICAL STRUCTURE

Do the tasks your teacher recommends.

When you describe a person, you have to make the same choices as when you describe a scene. You still have to decide how to order the points of your description according to their position or their order of importance. But there is one clear difference. You are more likely to have a personal reaction to a human being than to a table setting, an apartment, or some laboratory apparatus. From a person's physical appearance, you are likely to make judgments about his life and character. Everyone tends to make judgments about people based on first impressions—"love at first sight" is that type of spontaneous reaction. We look at people and we react to what we see. Compare these two sentences:

My uncle fiddles with his watch-chain and clears his throat before every sentence.

My uncle is so nervous that I can't stand being with him for long.

Which one tells more about the uncle and which one tells more about the writer?

As you write, consider whether you are describing the actual person or whether you are describing your reactions to that person. Decide which of the two is more useful and interesting for your reader.

1. Write a five-paragraph essay with the title: **American Gothic:** a Painting by Grant Wood.

   Here are some suggestions for the essay. You can, of course, use your own content, organized in whatever way you like.

   1. General introduction: describe the painting in very general terms—no details yet. Give an overview of what you see there.
   2. Description of the man: describe the man in detail—his physical appearance, his clothes, his expression.
   3. Description of the woman: describe the woman in detail—her appearance, her clothes, her expression.
   4. Description of the setting: describe the background, the buildings, the architectural features, the details.
   5. Your reactions and inferences: describe your reactions to the people in the painting. This part will obviously be colored by your own life, experiences, prejudices, and emotions. These questions might start you thinking:

      What kind of people are they?
      What kind of work do they do?
      What do they do in their spare time?
      Are they married?
      If so, are they happily married?
      Are they married to each other, or to two other people?
      Do they have any children? Grandchildren?
      Do they understand them?
      Are they strict? Permissive?
      Do they show their emotions?
      What country do they live in?
      Do they have a comfortable house?
      What do they do when people visit them?
      What do they feel about current issues in the news?
      Do they go to church?
      Do they gamble?
      What is their favorite book?
      Would you like them to be members of your family?

2. Describe in detail a member of your family, a friend, or someone you know well. Describe what the person looks like: features, hair, skin, figure, hands, feet, and clothes. If this person has **one** main characteristic, make sure that your description conveys it, even if you never say directly that the person is, for example, nervous, snobbish, or generous. Try to suggest that one important feature in the details you include. Ask another student to read your description and give a one-word title to sum up the person you have described.

3. Describe in detail someone that you do not know: someone you see on the street, in a bus or train, in a store, in a park, in a restaurant, or in your neighborhood. Add a paragraph noting what you infer about the person from his appearance. Can you make inferences about character, job, social status, tastes, hobbies, family, or daily routine? What do you consider to be the most important feature of the person? Where will you mention it in your description?

4. Go to a library and find a picture of Ernest Hemingway **or** of John Steinbeck in a book or encyclopedia. Describe his appearance in detail.

3

DESCRIBING A MOMENT

Focus on these syntactic structures

> agreement: **there is** and **there are**
> sentence division and punctuation
>> fragments and run-ons
>> **yes/no** questions
> modifiers
>> phrases (**with, -ing, on, in, at, of,**)
>> adjectives and adverbs
> capitals
> verbs: **-ing** continuous tenses
> clauses: **who, that**
> negatives: quantity words
> determiners: possessives
> **-ing** phrases
> sentence combining

Focus on these rhetorical structures

> organizing a description
>> spatial order
>> climactic order
> conveying a mood
> selecting details

INTRODUCTION

"I walked into the room and I saw . . ." "I turned on the TV and saw . . ." "My father walked in just as . . ." In everyday speech we describe moments that we want another person to share. We make our description as vivid as possible so that our listener will feel the same excitement, happiness, fear, or embarrassment that we did at the moment. A listener can interrupt and ask questions for more details: "What was she wearing?" A reader has to be content with what the writer gives him. So when you write a description of a memorable moment, remember that the reader is getting all the information second-hand, through you. The reader will get his picture of the setting, the details, and the mood from what you tell him. So give him an accurate, detailed picture.

CORE COMPOSITION

1. In the painting **Nighthawks,** (p. 32), Edward Hopper captures a moment, frozen in time. With some other students, discuss the picture—both what is shown (the facts) and what you infer. The following questions might help your discussion:

   What time of day or night is it?

   Where is it? In a city? In a small town?

   What country is it?

   What year is it?

   What time of year is it?

   What kind of people are they?

   What is their relationship to each other?

   Why are they in the coffee shop?

   What do you think happened just before and just after this moment? (Imagine that this is one scene from a movie.)

   What is the mood of the picture?

   Would you want to be a part of that scene at that moment? Why, or why not?

2. Individually, write one paragraph describing the moment captured by Hopper. Describe the place and the people and what the people are doing at the moment. Try also to convey the mood of that moment; is it, for example, lonely, strange, gloomy, happy? Describe the **details** that make you think of that mood when you look at the picture.

3. Exchange papers with another student. Add a one-word title to the other student's description; the word should describe the mood conveyed in

Edward Hopper, **Nighthawks.** Courtesy of The Art Institute of Chicago.

the writing. Examine your partner's paragraph. Ask yourself the questions below and write down your answers. With your partner, compare your two sets of answers.

Questions   What does the writer mention first? Last?

What does the writer see as the most important feature(s) of the picture?

What adjectives does the writer use to describe the scene and the people?

Does the writer mention the empty street? the empty store-front? the contrast of light and dark? If he does, what does he say about them?

Has the writer left out anything that you consider important?

Has the writer included anything that you left out?

FOCUS A: SYNTACTIC STRUCTURE

Do the tasks your teacher recommends.

• **1.** Task (group or individual)

Add **there is** or **there are** to the beginning of each of the following phrases to make them into complete sentences:

a. a lot of people on the beach

b. a lot of money on the table

c. nobody in the room

d. a bunch of flowers in the kitchen

e. some letters for you on the desk

f. some meat in the refrigerator

g. a friend of ours in that photograph

h. a letter from your parents in my bag

i. a picture of roses on the wall

j. a whole cake left

k. some good news in today's newspaper (the **-s** on **news** is not a plural **-s**)

l. a well-dressed woman with two shopping bags getting on the train now

Now write all of the sentences as **yes/no** questions. Change only the word order and do not leave out any words.

Example There is a loaf of bread on the plate.
Is there a loaf of bread on the plate?

• • 2. Task (individual)

Look carefully at a picture hanging on a wall in someone's home, in a store, or in an art gallery. Choose a picture that shows people in the middle of an activity. Describe the picture using **there is** and/or **there are** to introduce a few of your sentences. Think about what influences your decision to use **there is** or **there are.**

• • 3. Task (group or individual)

Fill in the blank spaces in the two sentences below with descriptive phrases beginning with **-ing, with, on, in, at,** etc., so that you distinguish between the two men in the picture **Nighthawks.**

The man _____ is sitting down.
The man _____ is sitting down, too.

(Two men are sitting down. Which one are you talking about?) Now write four more pairs of sentences to distinguish between people in your classroom. Look for similarities first, then differences.

Example The girl has brown hair.

(Which girl? More than one has brown hair.)

Your pair of sentences:

The girl with the red scarf around her neck has brown hair.

The girl sitting next to the window has brown hair, too.

• • 4. Task (group or individual)

Write answers to the questions below about Hopper's painting **Night-hawks** on p. 32. Use words like **probably, possibly, perhaps, maybe, might** in your answers to show that these are guesses. Which words in your answers need capital letters?

What language are the people speaking?
What month is it?
What city or town are the people in?
What is the nearest river?
What is the name of the coffee shop?
What is the name of the street?
What day of the week do you think it is?

• 5. Task (individual)

Make a list for a tourist, telling him where to go and what to do in any big town or city that you know well.

Example Go to the top of the Empire State Building.

Remember that names of streets, buildings, rivers, parks, monuments, etc., will have capital letters.

• 6. Task (individual)

Write ten sentences describing what you **were doing** at the given times yesterday. Use **was** + ——**ing** form of the verb.

Example At 9 o'clock I **was** eat**ing** breakfast.

(That is, you were in the middle of eating breakfast.)

7:00 a.m.	4:00 p.m.
9:00 a.m.	5:30 p.m.
10:30 a.m.	7:00 p.m.
12:00 noon	9:00 p.m.
2:00 p.m.	11:00 p.m.

• 7. Task (group or individual)

Use the **yes/no** question test (Task 2, pp. 6–7) to determine which of the sentences in the paragraph below are correctly punctuated and which are fragments or run-ons. Rewrite the passage and make fragments and run-ons into sentences.

There are a few words that can be used to **join** two sentences together. These are:

, and , but , or , so , nor , for , yet

She likes beef, but she never buys it.
Does she like beef? (but) Does she never buy it?

a. A woman is sitting alone in a coffee shop. **b.** Which looks very dismal. **c.** Two men are sitting there too they are both wearing hats. **d.** The counterman is wearing white clothes. **e.** Very clean-looking clothes. **f.** The woman is alone, however she doesn't look unhappy. **g.** Because there is a smile on her face. **h.** She wants to order a meal. **i.** To eat a sandwich, a salad, and some fruit. **j.** She will probably leave the coffee shop. **k.** As soon as she has finished her meal.

• • 8. Task (group or individual)

Write five base sentences (subject + predicate—see Tasks 1 and 2, pp. 6–7) describing the photograph, **Family** on p. 36.

Example The people look sad.

Now rewrite each sentence as a **yes/no** question.

Example Do the people look sad?

Now add something extra to the beginning of each sentence:

Examples At this moment, the people look sad.
As they look through the gates, the people look sad.

Vocabulary when; while; as;
hints because; -ing

Now rewrite each of your new sentences as a **yes/no** question.

Examples Do the people look sad at this moment?
Do the people look sad as they look through the gates?

Sara Cedar Miller, **Family.** Courtesy of Sara Cedar Miller.

•• **9.** Task (group or individual)

Write a list of **adjectives** that could describe the man and the two little girls in the **Family** photograph.

Examples tall, untidy, hopeful

Write a list of **adverbs** that could describe the way they are looking through the gate.

Examples casually, hopefully

• **10.** Task (group or individual)

There are two little girls in the **Family** photograph. Write sentences that include details that will tell your reader which girl you are talking about. Use the following patterns:

The little girl _____ is four years old.
The little girl _____ is two years old.

How many distinguishing features between the two girls can you find? Use them all in sentences in the above patterns.

Vocabulary who; with; -ing;
hints on; in

• **11.** Task (group or individual)

Complete the following sentences about the photograph **Family.**

a. The little girl who (that) is _____ looks about four years old.

b. The man, who is _____, looks as if _____.

Also complete the following sentences about the painting **Nighthawks** by Hopper on p. 32.

c. The man who (that) _____ looks as if _____.

d. The woman in the picture, who _____, might be
_____.

• **12.** Task (group or individual)

Combine the following pairs of sentences by making the **second** sentence of each pair into a clause introduced by **who**(m), **that,** or an omitted **who**(m) or **that.** Combine each pair in three ways.

Examples The girl is over there.
You met the girl last week.
1. The girl whom you met last week is over there.
2. The girl that you met last week is over there.
3. The girl you met last week is over there.

a. The man is her cousin's husband.
She has just insulted the man.

b. The student got the highest grade.
Everyone liked the student the best.

c. The little boy has broken two windows.
Two people are chasing the little boy.

• • **13.** Task (individual)

Write a description of the room in the photograph by Walker Evans on p. 16. Tell what the room does **not** contain. (From the photograph, imagine what the rest of the room looks like, what it contains and what it does not contain.)

Vocabulary hints not any; no; hardly any; few;
not much; not many

Examples There is not much comfort
There are no comfortable chairs.
There aren't any pillows.

• **14.** Task (group or individual)

Write sentences with an apostrophe (') to show possession. Use all the words listed below.

Examples woman—hair
The woman's hair is long.
The most vibrant part of the picture is the woman's hair.

In the picture **Nighthawks** (p. 32)
counterman—hat
men—hats
men—suits
woman—elbow

In the photograph **Family** (p. 36)
little girl—hair
man—coat

little girls—clothes
little girls—father

Now write sentences using the words below, using **of** instead of the apostrophe.

Example street—emptiness
The emptiness of the street shows that it must be late at night.

Nighthawks
stools—height
street lamps—light
window—size
two men at the counter—similarity

Family
people at the gate—expressions
little girl's jacket—thickness
pavement—pattern
gates—solidity

• • 15. Task (individual)

Examine the following uses of the **-ing** phrase. Notice what function it performs in the sentence. In the second sentence, for example, it tells the reader more about the man in the photograph **Family** on p. 36.

The people are **looking through the gates.**

The man **looking through the gates** is holding a child.

They all enjoy **looking through the gates.**

Looking through the gates is great fun.

Looking through the gates, the three people are waiting for somebody.

They never get tired of **looking through the gates.**

Choose one other **-ing** phrase from the following and practice using it in different sentence positions:

sitting in a coffee shop at night
eating alone
doing nothing

• 16. Task (group or individual)

Combine the groups of sentences below into **one** sentence only for each group. Keep the meaning the same. Some hints are given; try them all and choose the one you like the best.

Example   The woman looks stern.
The man looks stern.

The man and the woman look stern.
Both the man and the woman look stern.
The woman looks stern and so does the man.
The woman looks stern and the man does too.

a. The two men are sitting down.
The woman is sitting down.

and | and so

b. The two men are not standing up.
The woman is not standing up.

and . . . either |
neither . . . nor |
and neither |, nor

c. The picture is depressing.
The picture shows a deserted town.

which | -ing | of

d. The little girl is sitting on her father's shoulders.
She is sitting comfortably.
She is wearing a coat.
The coat is white.
The coat is furry.

who | -ing | in

e. The man has two daughters.
The daughters are little.
The man is looking through the gates.
The gates are made of iron.
The gates are locked.

with | who

FOCUS B: RHETORICAL STRUCTURE

Do the tasks your teacher recommends.

Describing a moment is like taking a photograph: the camera clicks, and the moment is recorded. Writing takes longer than a click, as all writers know, but it too can preserve a moment forever. Your reader will get his impression of a moment from the details you select and the features you emphasize. When you photograph a moment with a camera, you see it all and record it all in one second. When you describe that same moment in writing, you have to order your description, point by point, from a beginning to an end. The way you organize your points will affect the way your reader sees the moment. He will learn about the details one by one; he will see only what you choose to describe.

Your purpose for writing will help you decide which details to include. If you want to give a **total** picture of a scene then you will include all the details: you will then have to decide which detail to describe first and how the others follow. But when you decide that you want to emphasize one specific impression or to convey a mood of a scene, many of the details become unnecessary. In the drama of a street fight, for example, it is not necessary for the reader to know how many trees there are along the street. Selecting is an essential part of the writing process; it is in painting, photography and other arts, too.

1. Find any action snapshot of your family or friends—not a posed shot with everyone in a line smiling at the camera. Describe the moment that the photograph captures. Or find a picture in a magazine that shows people in the middle of doing something. Describe the details of the picture so that anyone reading your description without seeing the picture would be able to "see" the same scene. Let another student read your description and draw a rough sketch of where the people are and what they are doing, asking you questions when any details are not clear.

2. Write two or three paragraphs describing in detail what you see as you walk into a public place: a station, a classroom, a cafeteria, a party, or a dance-hall. Imagine that you have a camera with you and you take a picture as you walk in. (If you own a camera, you could actually take a picture and include it with your writing assignment.) Describe what you see as you walk in.

   Begin with:
   As I walk into _____, I see _____.

Spend time planning which details you will include and in which order you will describe them.

3. Choose **one** of the following and describe the **moment** of:

   a scientist finishing an experiment
   a surgeon concluding a successful, delicate operation
   a botanist discovering a rare flower
   an archeologist discovering a treasure-filled tomb
   a student finishing a term paper
   a young man or woman greeting his or her first date
   a child opening a present

   Give details about the person, the place, and the setting. Try to let your reader know how the person you are describing **feels:** what is the mood of the moment?

4. Read the passage below. Write your own description of observations you have while walking in a park, walking along a street, riding on a bus, or waiting in the main lobby of your school.

   Begin, as Updike does, by giving details of the time, place, and weather (if you are outside), and use chronological order. Use **-ing** forms. Notice how Updike's account can be reduced to a list:

There we saw:
rocks emerging

a pigeon strutting
a policeman getting his shoe wet
three relatives trying to coax a little boy

but he adds details to each item to make the scene come alive for his reader. Notice also that the "There we saw:" is necessary to make each item listed into a complete sentence.

March 1956

On the afternoon of the first day of spring, when the gutters were still heaped high with Monday's snow but the sky itself was swept clean, we put on our galoshes* and walked up the sunny side of Fifth Avenue to Central Park. There we saw:

Great black rocks emerging from the melting drifts, their craggy* skins glistening like the backs of resurrected* brontosaurs.*

A pigeon on the half-frozen pond strutting* to the edge of the ice and looking a duck in the face.

A policeman getting his shoe wet testing the ice.

Three elderly relatives trying to coax* a little boy to accompany his father on a sled ride down a short but steep slope. After much balking,* the boy did, and, sure enough, the sled tipped over and the father got his collar full of snow. Everybody laughed except the boy, who sniffled.

Four boys in black leather jackets throwing snowballs at each other. (The snow was ideally soggy,* and packed hard with one squeeze.)

Seven men without hats.

Twelve snowmen, none of them intact.

Two men listening to the radio in a car parked outside the Zoo; Mel Allen was broadcasting the Yanks-Cardinals game from St. Petersburg.

JOHN UPDIKE "Central Park"

*Gloss   galoshes rubber boots
craggy jagged, uneven
resurrected brought back to life
brontosaurs prehistoric beasts
strutting walking proudly, arrogantly
coax encourage
balking refusing
soggy soft and wet

4

DESCRIBING WHAT PEOPLE DO

Focus on these syntactic structures

> agreement: singular/plural
> verbs
>> present tense
>> past tense
> modifiers: frequency words (**often, always, sometimes,** etc.)
> sentence connectors: sequence (**first, next, then,** etc.)
> negatives
> noun plurals
> **-s** inflection
> sentence combining: **when, whenever, after, as soon as, once**

Focus on these rhetorical structures

> organizing a narrative: chronological order
> linking the steps in a sequence

INTRODUCTION

When you tell a friend how your brother spends his day at work, or when you tell your mother how your aunt makes chocolate cake, you are describing what people do. The activities happen one after the other, in sequence; the logical way to report them is in that same order in which they occurred (chronological order). In speech, your listener can question you if you leave anything out—"Doesn't she use any baking soda?"—but in writing you have to make sure that all the details are included, in order.

CORE COMPOSITION

INTERVIEW WITH TRUMAN CAPOTE

INTERVIEWER: What are some of your writing habits? Do you use a desk? Do you write on a machine?

CAPOTE: I am a completely horizontal author. I can't think unless I'm lying down, either in bed or stretched on a couch and with a cigarette and coffee handy. I've got to be puffing and sipping. As the afternoon wears on, I shift from coffee to mint tea to sherry to martinis. No, I don't use a typewriter. Not in the beginning. I write my first version in longhand (pencil). Then I do a complete revision, also in longhand. Essentially I think of myself as a stylist, and stylists can become notoriously obsessed* with the placing of a comma, the weight* of a semicolon. Obsessions of this sort, and the time I take over them, irritate me beyond endurance*. . . . Then I type a third draft on yellow paper, a very special certain kind of yellow paper. No, I don't get out of bed to do this. I balance the machine on my knees. Sure, it works fine; I can manage a hundred words a minute. Well, when the yellow draft is finished, I put the manuscript away for a while, a week, a month, sometimes longer. When I take it out again, I read it as coldly as possible, then read it aloud to a friend or two, and decide what changes I want to make and whether or not I want to publish it. I've thrown away rather a few short stories, an entire novel, and half of another. But if all goes well, I type the final version on white paper and that's that.

Writers at Work: The "Paris Review" Interviews, First Series,
ed. by MALCOLM COWLEY

*Gloss **notoriously obsessed**   famous for their concern
weight   importance
beyond endurance   more than I can bear

1. Read the interview with writer Truman Capote. In this excerpt, he de-

scribes how he writes. Think of an activity that you like to do and that you do well. Join up with another student. Tell each other about the activity you have chosen.

2. Choose one of you to be the interviewer; the other will be interviewed about his chosen activity. The interviewer will ask questions and make notes as the one being interviewed responds with a step-by-step description of how he performs the chosen task. The interviewer should continue to ask questions until he has in his mind—and in his notes—a clear picture of the steps in the activity.

3. Still in pairs, write a one-paragraph report from the notes made by the interviewer.
   Begin with:

   When X _____ (e.g. rides a motorcycle), she/he _____.

4. Change roles with your partner: the interviewer will now be interviewed. Repeat Tasks 2 and 3. Now you will have a paragraph about each of you.

5. With your partner, discuss the following questions about each of your paragraphs. Write down a set of answers for each paragraph and compare those answers.

Questions   In what order have you described the actions?

Have you used any expressions that indicate the time and sequence of events? (for example: **first, next, then, finally**)

Which words does Capote use to show time sequence?

How many steps are there in the sequence of Capote's writing process? Make a summary, in the form of a list, of what he does in his writing process:

1. He lies down
2. etc.

How many main steps are there in **your** description of your chosen activity?

Does your description emphasize those main steps?

Can you rewrite your paragraph as a list? Try it.

6. Individually, rewrite the paragraph describing your activity, using **I** instead of **he** or **she.**
   Begin with:

   When I _____ (e.g. ride a motorcycle), I _____.

Make all the necessary changes.

FOCUS A: SYNTACTIC STRUCTURE

Do the tasks your teacher recommends.

• 1. Task (group or individual)

Rewrite Capote's account of his writing habits (p. 44) from the point of view of the interviewer. Use the third person (**he**).
Begin with:

Capote <u>is</u> a completely horizontal author.
Make all other changes that are necessary and underline all the changes you make.

(§1) • 2. Task (group or individual)

Rewrite your account of the way Capote writes (in Task 1, above) as if you were a reporter writing fifty years from now. You will, therefore, use the past tense.
Begin with:

Capote <u>was</u> a completely horizontal author.
Underline all the changes you make.

• 3. Task (individual)

Go back to the account of an activity that you wrote about for the Core Composition in this chapter. Rewrite it in general terms, using **they.**
Begin with:

Whenever people _____ (e.g. ride a motorcycle), they _____.

Make all the necessary changes, and underline each change.

• 4. Task (group or individual)

Read Eldridge Cleaver's account of his daily routine in prison.

Folsum Prison
September 19, 1965

My day begins officially at 7:00, when all inmates are required to get out of bed and stand before their cell doors to be counted by guards who walk along the tier,* saying, "1, 2, 3 . . ." However, I never remain in bed until 7. I'm usually up by 5:30. The first thing I do is make my bed. Then I pick up all my books, newspapers etc.

off the floor of my cell and spread them over my bed to clear the floor for calisthenics.* . . . Still in the nude, the way I sleep, I go through my routine: kneebends, butterflies, touching my toes, squats, windmills. I continue for about half an hour. . . .

Usually by the time I finish my calisthenics, the trustee (we call him tiertender or keyman) comes by and fills my little bucket with hot water. . . . He pokes the spout [of his big bucket] through the bars and pours you about a gallon of hot water. . . .

When the guard has mail for me he stops at the cell door and calls my name, and I recite my number—A-29498—to verify that I am the right Cleaver. When I get mail, I avert my eyes so I can't see who it's from. Then I sit down on my bed and peep at it real slowly, like a poker player peeping at his cards. I can feel when I've got a letter from you, and when I peep up on your name on the envelope I let out a big yell. It's like having four aces. But if the letter is not from you, it's like having two deuces,* a three, a four, and a five, all in scrambled suits. . . . What is worse is when the guard passes my door without pausing. I can hear his keys jingling. If he stops at my door the keys sound like Christmas bells ringing, but if he keeps going they just sound like—keys. . . .

Well . . . after I've finished my calisthenics and the hot water has arrived, I take me a bird (jailbird) bath in the little sink. It's usually about 6:00 by then. From then until 7:30, when we are let out for breakfast, I clean up my cell and try to catch a little news over the radio. Radio?—each cell has a pair of earphones!—with only two channels on it. The programs are monitored from the radio room. The radio schedule is made up by the radio committee, of which I am a member.

At 7:30, breakfast. From the mess hall, every day except Saturday, my day off, I go straight to the bakery, change into my white working clothes, and that's me until noon. From noon, I am "free" until 3:20, the evening mandatory* lockup, when we are required, again, to stand before our cell doors to be counted. There is another count at 6:30 p.m.—three times every day without fail.

When I'm through working in the bakery, I have the choice of 1) going to my cell; 2) staying in the dining room to watch TV; 3) going down to the library; or 4) going out to the yard to walk around, sit in the sun, lift weights, play some funny games. . . .

On the average I spend approximately seventeen hours a day in my cell. I enjoy the solitude. The only drawback is that I am unable to get the type of reading material I want, and there is hardly anyone with a level head to talk to.

ELDRIDGE CLEAVER, **Soul on Ice**

*Gloss   **tier**   floor
  calisthenics   exercises
  deuces   twos
  mandatory   compulsory, required

Rewrite Cleaver's account as if you were a reporter writing about his daily routine.
 Begin with:

<u>Cleaver's</u> day begins officially at 7:00. <u>He</u> never <u>remains</u> in bed. . . .

Make all the necessary changes and underline each change.

• **5.** Task (individual)

Make a list of the times and the events of **your** daily routine. Include some details.

Example	Event	Details
	8:00—eat breakfast	orange juice, coffee, toast
	8:30—get dressed	blue jeans, shirt, sweater

Now rewrite your list as a connected paragraph, with the details included.

Vocabulary hints   Words to show how often: often; usually; always; sometimes; frequently; occasionally

Words to connect ideas: first; first of all; to begin with; second; then; next; finally; when; as soon as; after

Example   At 8 o'clock I eat breakfast. I usually have orange juice, coffee, and toast. Then I get dressed.

(§5) • **6.** Task (individual)

After Task 5 has been checked, rewrite it as if somebody else were writing about you. Use your own name and **he** or **she.** Remember the -s ending on verbs.

Example   At 8 o'clock she eats breakfast. She usually has orange juice, coffee, and toast. Then she gets dressed.

(§5) • • **7.** Task (individual)

Add to your list of daily activities (in Task 5) some activities that you **don't** do but wish you had time for.

Example sit and think
play baseball

Rewrite this new list as a paragraph. Add any details about the activities that will make your paragraph more interesting, and explain why you don't do them.

Vocabulary hints never; not ever; hardly ever; not often; seldom; rarely

• 8. Task (group or individual)

Write generalizations using a noun from column A and a verb from column B and add any other details to make the sentence interesting. Use **A(n)** and verb + **-s** in each sentence.

A	B
bank robber	fix
historian	deliver
journalist	steal
physicist	interpret
pharmacist	prepare
farmer	write
mechanic	experiment
obstetrician	cultivate

Example A bank robber steals money from a safe-deposit box if he can break it open.

Then rewrite your sentences using **all, most,** or **some** in place of **a.** Make all other necessary changes and underline them.

Most bank robbers steal money from safe-deposit boxes if they can break them open.

• 9. Task (group or individual)

Read the following paragraph by Oscar Lewis right through once, without stopping to work out the verb form.

The qualities looked for in a spouse (vary/varies) considerably between boys and girls. In selecting a wife, boys generally (choose/chooses) a girl for romantic reasons, beauty, or personality. Girls (tend/tends) to be more realistic about selecting a husband and will often (refuse/refuses) to marry a boy who is known to drink, chase women, be violent, or be lazy. However, status* factors are very important in marriage. It is usual for boys to (seek/

seeks) out a girl who is poorer and who (have/has) the same or less education, so that "the man can be boss" and his family need not be ashamed before her. Tepoztecan* boys (tend/tends) to "respect" and avoid having affairs with girls from the more important and prosperous* families, for fear of incurring reprisals* from the parents of such girls. Girls, on the other hand, (seek/seeks) to improve their economic status with marriage, and it is rare for a girl to (marry/marries) a man with less education. As a result of these attitudes, the daughters of the families in the upper economic group in the village (have/has) difficulty finding husbands. They (tend/tends) to marry later, and to marry more educated men or men from the outside. Occasionally a wealthy girl in her late twenties will marry a boy poorer than herself rather than (remain/remains) unmarried.

OSCAR LEWIS, **Life in a Mexican Village**

*Gloss **status**   social position
Tepoztecan   from the village of Tepoztlán, in Mexico
prosperous   wealthy, rich
incurring reprisals   causing acts of revenge

Now go back and circle the correct verb forms. Ask yourself each time: Is the subject of the verb singular or plural? The complete paragraph is in the Appendix on p. 168.

• 10. Task (group or individual)

Rewrite the paragraph by Oscar Lewis in Task 9 above, but write about a **boy, a girl,** and **a daughter.** Your second sentence will be:

In selecting a wife, a <u>boy</u> generally <u>chooses</u> a girl for romantic reasons, beauty or personality.

Make all the necessary changes and underline each change.

• • 11. Task (group or individual)

In the following description of how Hemingway writes, every seventh word has been omitted. Put an appropriate word in each blank space. A few have been done for you.

A working habit he has had _____ the beginning, Hemingway stands when he _____. He stands in a pair of _____ oversized loafers* on the worn skin _____ a Lesser Kudu*—the typewriter and _____ reading board chest-high opposite him.

_____ Hemingway starts on a project he _____ begins with a pencil, using the _____ board to write on onionskin typewriter _____. He keeps a sheaf of the _____ paper on a clipboard to the _____ of the typewriter, extracting the paper _____ sheet at a time from under _____ metal clip which reads, "These Must _____ Paid." He places the paper slantwise* _____ the reading board, leans against the _____ with his left arm, steadying the _____ with his hand, and fills the _____ with handwriting which through the years _____ become larger, more boyish, with a _____ of punctuation, very few capitals, and _____ the period marked with an x. _____ page completed, he clips it facedown _____ another clipboard which he places off _____ the right of the typewriter.

Hemingway _____ to the typewriter, lifting off the _____ board, only when the writing is _____ fast and well, or when the _____ is, for him at least, simple: _____, for instance.

He keeps track of _____ daily progress—"so as not to _____ myself,"—on a large chart made _____ of the side of a cardboard _____ and set up against the wall _____ the nose of a mounted gazelle* _____. The numbers on the chart showing _____ daily output of words differ from 450, 575, 462, 1250, _____ to 512, the higher figures on _____ Hemingway puts in extra work so _____ won't feel guilty spending the following _____ fishing on the Gulf Stream.

GEORGE PLIMPTON
Writers at Work: The "Paris Review" Interviews, Second Series,

*Gloss **loafers** casual shoes
Lesser Kudu type of animal, found in Africa
slantwise diagonally
a paucity of very little
shifts moves
dialogue conversation
kid fool (slang)
gazelle animal like an antelope

You will find the complete original passage in the Appendix on p. 169.

• 12. Task (group or individual)

Hemingway died in 1961. Rewrite Plimpton's description of how Hemingway wrote (in Task 11, above) in the past tense.
   Begin with:

Hemingway <u>stood</u> when he <u>wrote</u>.

Underline all the changes you make.

• 13. Task (group or individual)

From the complete passage about Hemingway by George Plimpton (in the Appendix on p. 169) make two lists of words that have the added -s ending.

Example	*noun plural* -s	*verb* -s
	loafers	stands
	years	writes

• • 14. Task (individual)

Refer to the accounts of how Capote and Hemingway write (p. 44 and p. 169). Then write ten sentences to describe what you personally do **not** do when you write.

Vocabulary hints never; not ever; hardly ever; not often; seldom; rarely

Examples I never write in bed.
I rarely use a clip-board.

• • 15. Task (group or individual)

Rewrite the following sentences, using **not** and another word to replace the word in bold type that begins with **n:**

Example She is going **nowhere** for her vacation.
She is**n't** going **anywhere** for her vacation.

  a. She eats **nothing** for lunch, so she is losing weight.
  b. She lives with **nobody.**
  c. She **never** speaks to people in the elevator.
  d. She invited **no one** in the building to her party.
  e. She has **no** pets.
  f. She has picked up **none** of her messages.
  g. She has contacted **neither** of her parents.

• 16. Task (group or individual)

Combine the following groups of sentences. Keep the meaning the same and write only **one** sentence for each group.

Vocabulary hints Words to combine all the given sentence groups: whenever; when; after; as soon as; once

Example The hot water has arrived.
I take a bath.
After (as soon as/once) the hot water has arrived, I take a bath.

a. The yellow draft is finished.
Capote puts the manuscript away for a while.

b. He takes it out again.
He reads it as coldly as possible.

c. I get mail.
I avert my eyes.

d. I'm through working in the bakery.
I have four choices.

e. I've finished my calisthenics.
The hot water has arrived.
I take a bath.

There is more than one way to combine each group of sentences. After you have tried some possibilities, you can check the passages about Capote (p. 44) and by Cleaver (p. 46) to find out what the author's choice was in each case.

FOCUS B: RHETORICAL STRUCTURE

Do the tasks your teacher recommends.

A secretary writes a job description. An anthropologist writes a research paper describing the customs of a primitive tribe. A salesman writes a report giving an account of how his customers behave when they see a new product. An applicant for a new job describes what he does in his present job. A nursing student writes a report of how patients with Parkinson's disease behave. A detective keeps a record of the daily routine of his suspect. When you describe what people do, clarity is very important. Your reader should have no gaps in his knowledge. He should have a clear picture of the sequence, the right order from start to finish. If you find you have to backtrack and say, "I forgot to mention before that . . ." then you are making your reader do the work that you, the writer and organizer, should have done. The result? You will probably lose your reader.

Getting the steps in the right order is just the beginning. Then you have to link the steps so that your narrative flows rather than jumps. Notice the difference when the words in parentheses in the following passage are left out:

The students arrive in September. (First,) they register for their chosen courses. (Then) they have a week or two to attend classes. (After that,) they can, if they want to, change their registration. (But) they have to pay.

1. In Eldridge Cleaver's account of his daily routine in prison (p. 46), notice the details he gives to help the readers form a clear picture of those uneventful days and of his own feelings about them. Write a detailed account of the daily routine of someone you know personally or of someone you know about. Make sure that the events are in chronological order and that they are linked to each other. Try to give details about some of the events so that your account becomes more than just a list. Cleaver tells the readers a great deal about getting mail; the expansion of the paragraph, the personal revelation, and the expression of emotion give the readers so much more than "On some days I get mail."

2. Interview someone in a job, for example, an elevator operator, a supermarket check-out clerk, a nurse, a short-order cook, or a waiter, and write an account of what that person does on a typical day on the job.

3. Read the passage by Oscar Lewis (p. 168) describing the choosing of a spouse in the Mexican village of Tepoztlán. Write two paragraphs describing how a. boys and b. girls in any city in any country proceed with **one** of the following activities:

choosing a career
choosing a spouse
choosing friends
arranging a first date

4. After you have filled in the blanks in the description of how Hemingway writes (p. 50) read the description again and then re-read the interview with Truman Capote (p. 42). Close your books and, with a partner, try to describe in your own words how both Capote and Hemingway write. Write one paragraph for each. Try to link the steps in each sequence.

5. The descriptions of Capote's and Hemingway's methods of writing emphasize different features: the Capote interview focuses on the author's actual process of writing and rewriting; Plimpton's account of Hemingway focuses on the writer's equipment, with details of the room, the implements, and the handwriting. Write an account of where and how **you**

write, what you use, what routine you follow, and what difficulties you encounter.

6. Choose **one** of the following and describe in detail what people do

when they vote for a Presidential candidate
when they give blood
when they celebrate the New Year in any country
when they train for a sports team
when they take a driving test
when they analyze a poem
when they apply for a visa or a passport

5

DESCRIBING WHAT HAPPENED

Focus on these syntactic structures

>verbs
>>past tense
>>present tense
>
>determiners
>>articles
>>quantity words
>
>modifiers
>>adjectives and adverbs
>>phrases
>
>clauses: **when, after, as soon as**
>sentence building and sentence combining

Focus on these rhetorical structures

>organizing a narrative: chronological order
>observing and reporting accurately
>adding details

INTRODUCTION

It would be almost impossible to get through a day without once describing "what happened." The next time you have a conversation with someone, notice when and why he describes past events. Writing includes a lot of description of past events, too. Your reader was not there to experience the events and learns only what you tell him. He will be much more interested in your account if he feels part of it and if you give him a full picture with accurate details. "Someone pushed me out of the line" does not give your listener or your reader much information. He wants to ask questions: Who pushed you? A man or a woman? What type of person? Was it someone you knew? Why did the person push you?

CORE COMPOSITION

1. In groups, discuss and write down in note form some details which could be added to the following skeleton outline of events to make it more interesting. Here you have a skeleton paragraph: the bare bones and no meat.

   Sam Spade came in at 3:40.
   He drank and smoked.
   At 4:30 the doorbell rang.
   Spade pressed the door-release button.

   As a part of an exciting detective novel, this passage would not capture the reader's attention. What details could be added? (Include the **ideas** of the skeleton sentences but not necessarily the actual sentences themselves.) For example, tell your reader more about the detective, Sam Spade:

   What did he look like?
   What was in his room?
   What rooms were there in his apartment?
   What kind of clock did he have?
   What were his movements inside his apartment?
   What did he drink and smoke?
   How much did he drink and smoke?
   How did he react when the bell rang?

2. From the notes you made, individually write a rough draft of a paragraph containing the events and details. Then read the passage on p. 59 from **The Maltese Falcon** by Dashiell Hammett. Compare its details to the ones you added. Whose version do you like best, yours or Hammett's? Why?

3. Here is another outline of events from a different passage of the same detective novel:

   Sam Spade answered the telephone.

He turned on the light.
It was five minutes past two.
He rolled a cigarette.
He lit it.
He took off his pajamas.
He got dressed.
He called for a taxi.

Individually, write three to four paragraphs that describe those events but with additional **details** so that the reader knows:

how often the phone rang
how Spade answered it
what he heard
what the room was like
what Spade was wearing
what tobacco he used
how he made a cigarette
what the weather was like
what Spade's clock was like
what one of his books was called
what kind of lighter he had
what his body was like
what clothes he put on
what number he called
what he put into his pockets

4. Compare your account with another student's and note how your specific details differ. As you read your partner's account, write answers to the following questions, discussing them with the writer if necessary.

Questions How many paragraphs did the writer write?

Did the writer include any conversation (with quotation marks)?

Did the writer use any adjectives that describe color, size, or texture?

Did the writer add details to each of the eight events in the outline?

Did the writer keep the order of events the same as in the outline? If not, why not?

5. Turn to pp. 169–171 for the original passage that the outline was made from. Read the whole passage through before you fill in words in the blanks. It will be hard for you to guess the author's exact choice each time, but you should be able to limit your choice to certain forms of words. For example, do you need an adjective, noun, verb, or adverb? Then compare Hammett's words with yours. Compare Hammett's details with your own.

6. With a small piece of paper, follow Spade's procedure of rolling a cigarette. Has Hammett described the action clearly and completely?

Spade's tinny alarm-clock said three-forty when he turned on the light in the suspended bowl again. He dropped his hat and over-coat on the bed and went into his kitchen, returning to the bed-room with a wine-glass and a tall bottle of Bacardi.* He poured a drink and drank it standing. He put bottle and glass on the table, sat on the side of the bed facing them, and rolled a cigarette. He had drunk his third glass of Bacardi and was lighting his fifth ciga-rette when the street-door-bell rang. The hands of the alarm-clock registered four-thirty. Spade sighed, rose from the bed, and went to the telephone box beside the bathroom door. He pressed the button that released the street-door-lock. He muttered, "Damn her," and stood scowling* at the black telephone-box, breathing irregularly while a dull flush grew in his cheeks.*

DASHIELL HAMMETT, **The Maltese Falcon**

*Gloss **Bacardi**   a brand of rum
scowling   frowning, making a face
dull flush grew in his cheeks   his face became red

FOCUS A: SYNTACTIC STRUCTURE

Do the tasks your teacher recommends.

• 1. Task (group or individual)

List all the past tense verb phrases in the two passages by Hammett (above and p. 170).

Example said
dropped
rose

Leave out all verb phrases that use an auxiliary, like **had (drunk)** or **was (lighting).** Concentrate on the one-word past tense form.

Next to each verb, write the beginning of a **yes/no** question, using **he, it,** or **they,** according to the context.

Example Did it say?
Did he drop?
Did he rise?

• 2. Task (group or individual)

Rewrite the passage by Hammett on p. 59 in present time. Stories are sometimes told in the present tense, as you will see in the story about Tootle the engine in the next chapter. Your first sentence will be:

Spade's tinny alarm-clock <u>says</u> three-forty when he <u>turns</u> on the light . . .

Underline the changes you make.

• 3. Task (group or individual)

Fill in **a, an** or **the** in the following sentences. If more than one choice in a sentence is possible, fill in both options. For example, when would a writer say, "He returned with **a** wine glass" and when would he say, "**the** wine glass"?

a. He turned on ＿＿ light in ＿＿ suspended bowl again.

b. He returned to ＿＿ bedroom with ＿＿ wine glass and ＿＿ tall bottle of Bacardi.

c. He rolled ＿＿ cigarette.

d. He stood scowling at ＿＿ black telephone box, breathing irregularly while ＿＿ dull flush grew in his cheeks.

e. He scowled at ＿＿ telephone on ＿＿ table while his hands took from beside it ＿＿ packet of brown papers.

f. The cold air brought with it half ＿＿ dozen times ＿＿ minute ＿＿ Alcatraz foghorn's dull moaning.

Now check your choices against Hammett's, p. 59 and p. 170.

• 4. Task (group or individual)

Answer the following questions about the two passages by Hammett. Use adverbs. Write complete sentences.

Example How was the alarm-clock mounted on the book?
The alarm-clock was mounted on the book **insecurely.**

a. How was the foghorn moaning?
b. How did Spade's thick fingers make a cigarette?
c. How did Spade's tweed overcoat hang on him?
d. How was Spade breathing?

- **5.** Task (group or individual)

  Combine each pair of sentences below into one sentence. Use an **adverb** in your sentence.

  Example He spoke. He was decisive.
  He spoke decisively.

  - **a.** He whispered. He was gentle.
  - **b.** He shouted. He was angry.
  - **c.** He insisted. He was stubborn.
  - **d.** He was running the meeting. He was democratic.
  - **e.** He offered his opinions. He was arrogant.
  - **f.** He argued. He was energetic.
  - **g.** He asked questions. He was forceful.
  - **h.** His opponents gave in. They were reluctant.
  - **i.** He looked around the room. He was jubilant.

- • **6.** Task (individual)

  Watch as someone does something: cooks a meal, changes a tire, or bathes a child, for example. As you watch, take notes so that you have a record of all the actions in sequence. Some time later, write a description of the activity using the **past tense.** Try to include some clauses introduced by **when, after,** and **as soon as** to combine some of the actions in the sequence.
  Notice the following:

  He **had drunk** his third glass of Bacardi **when** the bell rang.
  When it **had rung** three times bed-springs creaked.
  When he **had fastened** his shoes, he picked up the telephone.

(§6)• • **7.** Task (individual)

  Add some details to your description for Task 6, above. Use modifiers to add details about the person, about objects, or about how the person performed the action.
  Notice the following use of modifiers:

  Spade, **barefooted in green and white checked pajamas,** sat on the side of his bed.

  A white bowl **hung on three gilded chains** filled the room with light.

  He scowled at the telephone box, **breathing irregularly.**

• 8. Task (group or individual)

Rewrite the passage by Emily Post (p. 11) in the past tense. Imagine that you are a historian 500 years from now, describing breakfast in the twentieth century.
   Begin with:

More so than at other meals, there <u>was</u> a wide difference in the tastes of breakfast eaters.

Make all the necessary changes, underline them, and end with:

. . . and <u>made</u> each item easily accessible to everyone.

• 9. Task (group or individual)

Rewrite the passage by Oscar Lewis (p. 168) as if you were a historian in 3000 A.D. writing about ancient customs in a Mexican village.
   Begin with:

The qualities looked for in a spouse <u>varied</u> considerably between boys and girls.

Make any necessary changes and underline all the changes you make.

• • 10. Task (individual)

Imagine that you walked in to the movie **High Noon** at the point shown in the picture on p. 19. Describe what might have happened in the movie in the next fifteen minutes. You can either **a.** read a summary of the movie plot in a film encyclopedia to get an outline of the plot; or **b.** use your imagination! Use the past tense.

Example He walked toward his three enemies, and then . . .

• • 11. Task (group or individual)

After you have read through the following passage by Joan Didion, add articles **a, an** or **the** in each blank space. If more than one choice is possible in a sentence, fill in both options. Consider how the writer's meaning would change according to which one was chosen. Look at these two sentences, for example:

Maria always shopped for a household.
Maria always shopped for the household.

Both are possible—but with the second sentence the writer would expect the reader to know of one specific household she was referring to.

She had watched them in supermarkets and she knew ____ signs. At seven o'clock on ____ Saturday evening they would be standing in ____ checkout line reading ____ horoscope in **Harper's Bazaar** and in their carts would be ____ single lamb chop and maybe two cans of cat food and ____ Sunday morning paper, ____ early edition with ____ comics wrapped outside. They would be very pretty some of ____ time, their skirts ____ right length and their sunglasses ____ right tint and maybe only ____ little vulnerable* tightness around ____ mouth, but there they were, one lamb chop and some cat food and ____ morning paper. To avoid giving off* ____ signs, Maria shopped always for ____ household, gallons of grapefruit juice, quarts of green chile salsa,* dried lentils* and alphabet noodles, rigatoni* and canned yams,* twenty-pound boxes of laundry detergent. She knew all ____ indices* to ____ idle* lonely, never bought ____ small tube of toothpaste, never dropped ____ magazine in her shopping cart. ____ house in Beverly Hills overflowed with sugar, corn-muffin mix, frozen roasts and Spanish onions. Maria ate cottage cheese.

JOAN DIDION, Play It As It Lays

The original passage is on p. 171.

*Gloss **vulnerable** easily hurt, weak
giving off showing
salsa sauce
lentils small peas
rigatoni Italian pasta
yams sweet potatoes
indices signs, indications
idle unemployed, lazy

• **12.** Task (individual)

Write an account of what you or someone in your family bought when you last went shopping for food for a lot of people. Use the past tense. Do not specify exact amounts (one, two, three, etc.) but describe general quantities (some, a great deal of, etc.; see the list of quantity words in Task 6, p. 10).

•• **13.** Task (group or individual)

Add details to the following base sentences:
a. Birds are flying.
b. The child fell asleep.
c. A man eats.

    d. People sleep.

    e. The president is optimistic.

    f. Dogs bark.

Example The bottle is full.

The wine bottle in the middle of the table is full of homemade wine.

Or you could add even more details:

The large green wine bottle standing in the middle of the round mahogany table is full of homemade rhubarb wine that his girl-friend's mother makes in her cellar every year just before Thanksgiving.

You might find it helpful to ask some questions about the sentences:

What?	What is the bottle full of?
What kind of?	What kind of bottle/table/wine is it?
Where?	Where is the bottle? Where is the wine made?
Who?	Who makes the wine?
When?	When does she make the wine?

• • 14. Task (group or individual)

Add details to the following base sentences in the slots indicated. Refer to Task 13, above, for a list of questions that might help you to think of details. Use a word, a phrase, or a clause in each slot. Fill one slot at a time, as in the examples.

    a. The _____ men _____ signed the document _____

    b. _____ the _____ bomb exploded _____

    c. _____ prices _____ rise _____

    d. _____ the _____ manager hired the _____ woman _____

Examples _1_ the _2_ boy _3_ kissed _4_ the _5_ girl _6_

Possible fillers for each of the numbered slots are listed below.

1. Yesterday evening, the boy kissed the girl.
   Although he was shaking all over, the boy kissed the girl.
2. The timid boy kissed the girl.
3. The boy with the glasses kissed the girl.
   The boy who had not danced all evening kissed the girl.

4. The boy kissed and hugged the girl.

5. The boy kissed the beautiful girl.

6. The boy kissed the girl passionately.
The boy kissed the girl because he wanted to.
The boy kissed the girl who was engaged to the star boxer of the school.

• **15.** Task (group or individual)

Combine the following groups of sentences. Keep the meaning the same and write only **one** sentence for each group. Find as many ways as you can to combine the sentences and then choose the method you like the best.

a. Spade's alarm-clock said 3:40.
The alarm-clock was tinny.
Spade turned on the light again.

b. He dropped his hat on the bed.
He dropped his overcoat on the bed.
He went into his kitchen.
He returned to the bedroom.
He returned with a wine glass and some Bacardi.

c. A switch clicked.
A bowl filled the room with light.
The bowl was white.
The bowl was hung on three chains from the ceiling.

d. He scowled at the telephone.
The telephone was on the table.
His hands took a packet of papers.
The papers were brown.
His hands took a sack of Bull Durham.
They took them from beside the telephone.

e. He fastened his shoes.
He picked up the telephone.
He called Graystone 4500.
He ordered a taxicab.

f. The street doorbell rang.
He stuffed tobacco into his pockets.
He stuffed keys into his pockets.
He stuffed money into his pockets.

Check pp. 59 and 170 to see which choice Hammett made.

FOCUS B: RHETORICAL STRUCTURE

Do the tasks your teacher recommends.

When you write a letter, a report, or a college paper, you will often describe what happened. What is important to your reader is clarity. He should be able to read your narrative and know in which order the events occurred; did one event cause another or did it just happen before it? He should also be able to understand the purpose of this narrative in your piece of writing. A writer decides to describe what happened with one of several purposes in mind: he might want simply to tell a story or give information, or he might use the incident to illustrate and support a point he is making. A student, for example, might want to explain the causes and effects of a historical incident, but first he has to summarize what happened; a nurse might report on a patient's behavior during the night so that the day nurse has a full case history; a salesman or store manager might describe the activities of the past year in order to make recommendations for the next year; a scientist might write up a laboratory experiment for publication in a journal. In all of these writing situations, the writer's main purpose is to inform the reader of what happened before he himself comments on the events.

In a description of a sequence of past events, pay special attention to the time sequence. Organize the events chronologically before you write your account, so that you don't leave out any crucial event and have to write, "I should have said before that. . . ." Avoid wild leaps from one time to another, especially from past time to present time. Otherwise, your reader won't know where he is.

1. The two paragraphs below present a skeleton outline of events:

I rented a room at a motel. Almost everything in the room was plastic. Many things in the restaurant were plastic, too.

I returned to my room. I wanted a drink because I was depressed. Everything in the bathroom was sterilized. I reacted violently to the plastic, sterilized environment. Then I took a bath.

Add details to the events to expand the paragraphs and make them more interesting. Your details might include responses to the questions below. Write two new paragraphs based on the same events; use the events but do not use the actual sentences in the outline paragraphs above. You might begin:

In May 1974, as I was driving through California, I decided to stop for a night at a motel instead of just sleeping on the back seat of my truck. So . . .

I rented a room at a motel.
(Where? Was it expensive? Was there a sign outside?)

Almost everything in the room was plastic.
(Which items in the room were made of plastic? Which were not?)

Many things in the restaurant were plastic, too.
(What did you see there that was made of plastic?)

I returned to my room. I wanted a drink because I was depressed.
(Why were you depressed? What did you drink? Do you usually drink alone?)

Everything in the bathroom was sterilized.
(What items were sterilized? How did you know? What did they look like?)

I reacted violently to the plastic, sterilized environment. Then I took a bath.
(What did you do? How much water did you use? Hot or cold? How did you feel?)

Compare your description and your details with the passage from John Steinbeck's **Travels with Charley** on p. 171.

2. Individually, make a list of a skeleton outline of a sequence of actions that you took part in, college registration or applying for a job, for example. Do not include any details; just list the events. Then exchange papers with another student and add questions to your partner's skeleton outline, asking for more detailed information, as in Task 1, above. Exchange papers again and add details to your original outline in answer to your partner's questions. Expand your original outline into a detailed account of one to two paragraphs.

3. Use library resources (encyclopedias, books, newspapers, periodicals) to help you write a narrative account of the events comprising **one** of the following:

man's first landing on the moon
the lowering of the voting age in the U.S.A. from 21 to 18
the discovery of the cause of puerperal fever
Custer's last stand
the painting of the Sistine Chapel ceiling
Paul Revere's ride
The Boston Tea Party

4. Write a description of what happened in the most exciting class hour in school you have ever experienced. Describe it in detail so that your reader will be able to experience the excitement you felt.

6

MAKING A POINT

Focus on these syntactic structures

> verbs
>> past tense
>> future tense
>> present tense
>> forms (base, **-ing,** participle)
> sentence division and punctuation
> **-s** inflection
> **-ed** inflection
> sentence combining

Focus on these rhetorical structures

> narrating a sequence of events for a purpose
> making a generalization from personal experience
> illustrating a point with an incident

NTRODUCTION

When you tell someone a story about an event in your life, you know why you are telling that story, and you let your listener know why. For example, you tell a story about waiting at the bus stop in order to explain why you were late for class. You tell a story about walking home late at night to tell your listener why you think city life is dangerous. In writing, you will often use a narrative of past events. You will tell a story not just because it is a good story but because it helps you to make a point.

CORE COMPOSITION

1. Describe an incident from your childhood that means a lot to you, one that you will probably tell your own children about. Include details so that your reader will be able to picture the incident just as you experienced it.
   Begin with:

   Once, when I was little . . . ,

   and write one long paragraph. Use the simple past tense for a sequence of past events, such as:

   Everyone **left.** Then I **arrived** at the party!

   Use **had** + participle to express a time before a specific event in the past:

   When I **arrived** at the party, everyone **had** (already) **left.**

   (Compare this with how you would feel if this happened:
   When I arrived at the party, everyone left.)

2. Add another paragraph to the beginning or the end of your account of the incident and in it explain the importance and significance of the event for you **now.**
   Consider the following questions:

   Why do you remember it?

   When do you usually recall it?

   What can another person learn from it about your life?

   Can another person learn anything from it about life or people in general?

   Use the present tense in this paragraph to describe what you remember, think, and feel at the present moment.

3. Read quickly through the story "One Afternoon in 1939" on p. 70. The story has blank spaces in it. Don't work out each one; just get the idea of the events. Then close this book and write a summary of the story. Try to

remember as many details as you can. Then compare your summary with another student's.

4. With another student, fill in the verb forms in the story. When you think of two or more alternatives, write those down too and see if you can guess which word the author chose. Check the tense of the verbs you filled in (present or past?) and see if yours are the same as those in the original story, on p. 172. With your partner discuss where and why Brautigan switches tense from present to past and back again.

5. Check your own use of verb tenses in the description you wrote of your own childhood incident and of your feelings about the incident now. How many times have you switched from present to past or past to present?

6. Examine your two paragraphs again and write answers to the following questions:

Questions How many actual steps (actions) are there in your account of the incident? Make a list.

Did you describe the events in the order in which they actually happened (chronological order)? If not, what order did you use?

How many sentences did you write in your description of the incident (your first paragraph)?

How many sentences did Brautigan write from "Once when I was a little kid . . ." to ". . . wild flowers for food"?

Which sentences in the story by Brautigan tell of a new event and which ones give details about an event mentioned previously? Make two lists: events and details.

In your first paragraph describing the incident, which sentences add details?

Fill in an appropriate verb. Fit it in to the meaning, tone, and grammar of the story.

ONE AFTERNOON IN 1939

This is a constant story that I keep telling my daughter who _____ four years old. She _____ something from it and _____ to hear it again and again.

When it's time for her to _____ to bed, she _____, "Daddy, tell me about when you _____ a kid and climbed inside that rock."

"O.K."

She _____ the covers about her as if they _____ controllable clouds and _____ her thumb in her mouth and _____ at me with listening blue eyes.

70

"Once when I was a little kid, just your age, my mother and father _____ me on a picnic to Mount Rainier. We _____ up there in an old car and _____ a deer standing in the middle of the road.

We _____ to a meadow where there _____ snow in the shadows of the trees and snow in the places where the sun did not _____.

There _____ wild flowers growing in the meadow and they _____ beautiful. In the middle of the meadow there _____ a huge round rock and Daddy _____ over to the rock and _____ a hole in the center of it and _____ inside. The rock was hollow like a small room.

Daddy _____ inside the rock and sat there _____ out at the blue sky and the wild flowers. Daddy really _____ that rock and _____ that it was a house and he _____ inside the rock all afternoon.

He got some smaller rocks and _____ them inside the big rock. He _____ that the smaller rocks were a stove and furniture and things and he _____ a meal, _____ wild flowers for food."

That's the end of the story.

Then she looks up at me with her deep blue eyes and _____ me as a child playing inside a rock, _____ that wild flowers are hamburgers and _____ them on a small stove-like rock.

She can never _____ enough of this story. She _____ it thirty or forty times and always _____ to hear it again.

It's very important to her.

I think she uses this story as a kind of Christopher Columbus door to the discovery of her father when he was a child and her contemporary.

RICHARD BRAUTIGAN, Revenge of the Lawn

FOCUS A: SYNTACTIC STRUCTURE

Do the tasks your teacher recommends.

• 1. Task (group or individual)

Read the following passage.

Tootle the Engine (text by Gertrude Crampton, pictures by Tibor Gergely) is a popular and in many ways charming volume in the "Little Golden Books" series. It is a cautionary* tale even though it appears to be simply one of the many books about anthropomorphic* vehicles—trucks, fire engines, taxicabs, tugboats, and so on—that are supposed to give a child a picture of real life. Tootle is a young engine who goes to engine school, where two main lessons are taught: stop at a red flag and "always stay on the track no matter what." Diligence* in the lessons will result in the young engine's growing up to be a big streamliner. Tootle is obedient for a while and then one day discovers the delight of going off the tracks and finding flowers in the field. This violation* of the rules cannot, however, be kept secret; there are telltale traces* in the cowcatcher.* Nevertheless, Tootle's play becomes more and more of a craving,* and despite warnings he continues to go off the tracks and wander in the field. Finally the engine schoolmaster is desperate.* He consults the mayor of the little town of Engineville, in which the school is located; the mayor calls a town meeting, and Tootle's failings are discussed—of course Tootle knows nothing of this. The meeting decides on a course of action, and the next time Tootle goes out for a spin* alone and goes off the track he runs right into a red flag and halts. He turns in another direction only to encounter another red flag; still another—the result is the same. He turns and twists but can find no spot of grass in which a red flag does not spring up, for all the citizens of the town have cooperated in this lesson.

Chastened* and bewildered* he looks toward the track, where the inviting green flag of his teacher gives him the signal to return. Confused by conditioned reflexes* to stop signs, he is only too glad to use the track and tears happily up and down. He promises that he will never leave the track again, and he returns to the roundhouse* to be rewarded by the cheers of the teachers and the citizenry and the assurance that he will indeed grow up to be a streamliner.

DAVID RIESMAN, **The Lonely Crowd**

°Gloss **cautionary** warning, telling people to be careful
anthropomorphic with human personality
diligence care and hard work
violation breaking
telltale traces revealing marks
cowcatcher metal bars in front of engine to push cows off the tracks
craving strong wish
desperate hopeless
out for a spin out for a ride
chastened disciplined, scolded
bewildered confused
conditioned reflexes learned, automatic responses
roundhouse round building for storing locomotive engines

Notice that Riesman's account of the story of Tootle is written in the present tense. This is sometimes used to tell a story. The past tense is often used, too. Rewrite the story of Tootle in the past.
   Begin with:

Tootle <u>was</u> a young engine who <u>went</u> to engine school.

Make any other necessary changes. Underline all the changes you make.

• 2. Task (group or individual)

Rewrite the story of Tootle (in Task 1, above) as if it has not happened yet but will happen at some time in the future.
   Begin with:

Tootle <u>will go</u> to engine school, where two main lessons . . .

Make any other necessary changes. Underline all the changes you make.

• • 3. Task (group or individual)

Discuss with a group of students what point the Tootle story (in Task 1, above) is making. (In what way is it a "cautionary" tale? What is it cautioning its readers against? What are children expected to learn from it? What point is it making about society? Would you like your children or your younger brothers and sisters to read this story? Why or why not?)
   Write a short paragraph that tells the reader what point the story makes. Use the present tense throughout.

• 4. Task (group or individual)

Rewrite Brautigan's story, "One Afternoon in 1939," (p. 172) using the narrative present tense, the same tense that is used in the story of Tootle in Task 1, above. Rewrite only the part from "We came to a meadow . . ." to ". . . using wild flowers for food."
   Begin with:

We <u>come</u> to a meadow . . .

Make any other necessary changes. Underline all the changes you make.

• 5. Task (group or individual)

Make three lists of words with **-s** and **-ed** endings from the story "One Afternoon in 1939" on p. 172.

noun plural -s

Example years

verb -s *(present tense)*

Example gets

verb -ed *(simple past tense)*

Example climbed

• 6. Task (group or individual)

Use the **yes/no** question test (Task 2, pp. 6–8) to determine which of the following are sentences, which are fragments, and which are run-ons. Rewrite any fragments or run-ons as complete, correctly punctuated sentences.

Examples She gets something from it. (This is a sentence.) Does she get something from it?

And wants to hear it again. (This is a fragment; there is no subject.)

Rewrite it as:
And she wants to hear it again. or She gets something from it and wants to hear it again.

a. When it's time for her to go to bed.

b. She asks me to tell her a story.

c. She puts her thumb in her mouth, she looks at me.

d. Once when I was a little kid.

e. My mother and father took me on a picnic.

f. We drove up there in an old car we saw a deer standing in the middle of the road.

g. We came to a meadow where there was snow in the shadows of the trees.

h. There were wild flowers growing in the meadow they looked beautiful.

i. Daddy walked over to the rock and found a hole in the center of it.

j. The rock was hollow.

k. Like a small room.

i. Daddy sat inside the rock.

m. Staring out at the blue sky and the wild flowers.

n. Daddy really liked that rock, he pretended that it was a house.

• • 7. Task (individual)

Make **yes/no** questions from all the sentences you wrote in the Core Composition of this chapter to describe a childhood incident.

• • 8. Task (group or individual)

The following is the beginning of a paragraph by James Thurber. He makes a generalization about women (present tense) and this is followed by a humorous incident to illustrate the point he has made (past tense).

Another reason I hate women (and I am speaking, I believe, for the American male generally) is that in almost every case, where there is a sign reading "Please have exact change ready," a woman never has anything smaller than a ten-dollar bill. She gives ten-dollar bills to bus conductors and change-men in subways and other such persons who deal in nickels and dimes and quarters. Recently . . .

JAMES THURBER, "The Case Against Women"

Discuss with other students what kind of incident could follow the "Recently . . ." to illustrate the point that women never have small change. Then, individually, write an incident that could complete the paragraph. Use the past tense. The complete original paragraph is on p. 173. Notice how the present tense is used for generalizations at the beginning and end, and the past tense is used for the past-time incident.

• • 9. Task (individual)

Write a paragraph with a generalization followed by an incident to support the generalization. Notice how Thurber (p. 173) uses exaggeration to achieve a humorous effect.

Begin with **one** of the following:

One reason I hate
  bus drivers
  dog owners
  teachers   } is that
  nurses
  bank tellers
  TV newsmen

Use present tense for generalizations and past tense for the incident.

• 10. Task (group or individual)

Complete the following verb sequences with an appropriate form of the given verb, e.g., write, writing, or written. If two forms are possible, give them both and then write two sentences showing how these two different forms are used:

(write)	(design)	(see)
might _____	is being _____	has _____
should have _____	have _____	would have _____
could be _____	have been _____	is _____
did _____	will be _____	has been _____
was _____	do _____	would _____

•• 11. Task (group or individual)

Add capital letters and punctuation to the following two passages:

When I first took up my abode* in the woods that is began to spend my nights as well as days there which by accident was on independence day or the fourth of july 1845 my house was not finished for the winter but was merely a defence against the rain without plastering or chimney the walls being of rough weather-stained boards with wide chinks* which made it cool at night

HENRY DAVID THOREAU, **Walden**

*Gloss **abode** home
        chinks gaps, spaces

That was the thing about french girls and german girls there was not all this talking you couldnt talk much and you did not need to talk it was simple and you were friends he thought about france and then he began to think about germany on the whole he had liked germany better he did not want to leave germany he did not want to come home still he had come home he sat on the front porch

ERNEST HEMINGWAY, "Soldier's Home"

How many sentences did you make in each passage? Check p. 174 for the authors' punctuation, and count the number of sentences in each passage.

• **12.** Task (group or individual)

The following sentences from students' essays have a few errors in them that the students missed when editing. Write out the sentences with the errors corrected.

a. There is a lot of memories to remember as you get older.

b. One day me and my two cousins traveled to another place.

c. My cousin, although he was worried about us, he didn't lose his temper.

d. She was crying she thought I had been kidnapped.

e. I saw a beautiful doll dress in blue.

f. My mother sent me to my aunt house.

g. When I open the gift, I saw the most beautiful doll in the world.

h. My parents took my sisters and I to a playground where there was all kinds of games.

i. I felt that a lot of people want me to come out of that hospital.

• **13.** Task (group or individual)

Combine the following groups of sentences. Keep the meaning the same and write only **one** sentence for each group. Find as many ways as you can to combine the sentences and then choose the method you like the best.

a. We came to a meadow.
There was snow.
The snow was in the shadows of the trees.

b. This is a constant story.
I keep telling my daughter the story.
She is four years old.

c. Tootle is a young engine.
Tootle goes to engine school.
Two main lessons are taught there.

d. The schoolmaster consults the mayor of Engineville.
Engineville is a little town.
The school is located in Engineville.

e. Tootle is chastened.
Tootle is bewildered.
He looks toward the track.
There the flag of the teacher gives him the signal to return.

The flag is inviting.
The flag is green.

You can check the passages on p. 172 and p. 71 to see which choices Brautigan and Riesman made.

FOCUS B: RHETORICAL STRUCTURE

Do the tasks your teacher recommends.

"So what?" a reader might ask himself after reading a description of a scene, person, moment, or sequence of events. "Why is the writer telling me all this?" Writing should have a purpose. In real life, only novelists, journalists, and short story writers write simply because they have a story to tell. Other writers write to give information and to make a point. When college students write a paper, their main purpose might be to pass the course, but to do so they will have to make points about the subject matter and discuss those points with the knowledge gained from studying the material. We all try to see patterns in people and in events; we all make generalizations from our everyday experiences and from our reading. In writing we share these generalizations with our readers. When **you** write, your reader should know where your generalizations come from. If your point is not clear in your description or narration, then you should state it directly. Don't let your reader struggle to find your point—help him. Either begin with the point you want to make and then tell a story to illustrate it, as Thurber did (p. 173). Or begin with the incident and then draw a point from it, as Brautigan did (p. 172). The story you tell from your personal experience will make it clear to your reader why you hold the opinion you express.

1. Write down in a paragraph, in chronological order, the events of a children's story that you used to hear or read when you were a child—for example, "Little Red Riding Hood" or "Cinderella." Use the past tense for this narrative. Make sure that the events in this paragraph are described in the order in which they happened.

   Now add a second paragraph which makes a point about what children learn from the story about people and the way they behave. Use the present tense in this paragraph as you write generalizations about children and people.

2. Read the paragraph by James Thurber on p. 173 in the Appendix. Write down, in one sentence, an opinion (not a fact) that you hold about the opposite sex. Think of an incident that will illustrate this opinion. Write a paragraph including both the incident and your opinion. Decide which of the two you prefer to put first. After you have written your paragraph,

change the order and rewrite it the other way; how does the effect of your paragraph change when you move the sentence that expresses the opinion? Which order do you like the best? Give your paragraphs to another student and ask which one he likes the best.

3. Write a day-by-day journal for the next two days. In it, record all the major events of each day: what you did, where you went, what happened to you, what you ate, whom you met, etc. At the end of the two days, select one or two incidents, describe them in detail and make a point about them so that the reader knows why you selected them and why they are meaningful to you.

4. Discuss the following poem with other students.

STEP ON HIS HEAD

Let's step on daddy's head shout
the children my dear children as
we walk in the country on a sunny

summer day my shadow bobs dark on
the road as we walk and they jump
on its head and my love of them

fills me all full of soft feelings
now I duck with my head so they'll
miss when they jump they screech

with delight and I moan oh you're
hurting you're hurting me stop and
they jump all the harder and love

fills the whole road but I see it run
on through the years and I know
how some day they must jump when

it won't be this shadow but really
my head (as I stepped on my own
father's head) it will hurt really

hurt and I wonder if then I will
have love enough will I have love
enough when it's not just a game?

JAMES LAUGHLIN

What happens?
Why does the poet think it is important?
What point does the poet make from the incident?

Write an essay of three of four paragraphs. Use the same title as the poem. A suggested outline follows:

A. Summary of the incident the poet witnessed.

B. Summary of the point the poet made from the incident.

C. Your reaction to that point: do you agree or disagree with the poet's prediction? Why, or why not? Include in this paragraph one sentence that summarizes your own point of view.

D. Description of an incident from your own experience or reading that will illustrate and support your point of view.

7

SUPPORTING A POINT

Focus on these syntactic structures

> verbs
>> future tense
>> past tense
>> present tense
> sentence division and punctuation
>> fragments
>> **yes/no** questions
>> subject and verb
> clauses: **because**
> modifiers: frequency words
> sentence connectors: example (**for example, for instance**)
> verb phrases
>> verb + **to** + base form of verb
>> verb + **ing** form of verb
> parallel structures
> sentence combining

Focus on these rhetorical structures

> organizing a paragraph: beginning or ending with a generalization
> using examples, incidents, or facts
> writing a topic sentence
> addressing an audience

INTRODUCTION

When you make a point, it is important for your listener or reader to know why you are making it. If, for example, you say, "Nobody should go to college," you cannot expect everyone to accept that just because you said it—even if you said it three or four times! You need to say **why** you think that. You might give different reasons to a group of high school students or to a group of college professors, but whoever your audience is, you do need to state the reasons you have for making your point.

CORE COMPOSITION

_____. The woodshop was used to manufacture stocks for "homemades"* after Macy's stopped selling zip-guns.* We went from classroom to classroom answering "here," and trying to be "good." The math class was generally permitted to go to the gym after roll call. English was still a good class. Partly because of a damn good, tough teacher named Miss Beck, and partly because of the grade-number system (7-1 the smartest seventh grade and 7-12, the dumbest). Books were left in school, there was little or no homework, and the whole thing seemed to be a holding operation* until high school. Somehow or other, I passed the entrance exam to Brooklyn Technical High School. But I couldn't cut the mustard,* either academically or with the "American" kids. After one semester, I came back to PS 83, waited a semester, and went on to Benjamin Franklin High School.

> JACK AGUEROS, "Halfway to Dick and Jane: A Puerto Rican Pilgrimage"

*Gloss **homemades** guns made at home
        zip-guns small guns
        holding operation a way to pass the time
        cut the mustard reach the required standard

1. In small groups of three or four students, discuss what the paragraph by Jack Agueros is about. What is the writer trying to prove to you? What point is he making? How does he go about trying to prove his point? Is his writing formal or informal? What type of audience is he writing for?

2. The two opening sentences of the paragraph have been omitted. Supply two sentences that would sum up the ideas expressed in the paragraph and that would give the reader a preview of the content of the paragraph.
   Make a list (points 1, 2, 3, etc.) of the examples Agueros gives to support his point.

On page 174 in the Appendix you will find the actual opening sentences that Agueros wrote. How similar were yours to the original?

3. Still in small groups, write down some opinions that you hold on any topic.

Examples   The first day at a new school is a nightmare.
Chuan Hong is the best Chinese restaurant I know.

In everyday life, we often express an opinion like this and then go on to say why we think so, even if our audience does not challenge us. We go on to say what makes Chuan Hong so good: we describe the dishes, the service, the atmosphere, the clientele, the prices, and the friendly owner. We might compare and contrast it to other restaurants, too. In writing, this supporting of a point is necessary if we want a reader to accept our point of view.

4. Write a numbered list of examples, incidents, or facts to support all the opinion sentences (topic sentences) your group has chosen.

5. Individually, choose **one** of the sentences and write a paragraph containing the opinion sentence (topic sentence) and some reasons you have for holding that opinion. Support your opinion with examples, incidents, or facts.

Vocabulary   for example; for instance;
hints   to illustrate this

6. Exchange papers with a student in your group. Read your partner's paragraph and ask the following questions about it. Write answers to the questions and then discuss your answers with your partner.

Questions   How many examples, incidents, or facts did the writer give?

Do all the examples support the opinion expressed by the paragraph?

Which sentence is the topic sentence of the paragraph?

Where is the topic sentence in the paragraph: which sentence is it: first, second, etc., last?

Is the topic sentence restricted enough so that the writer really can support it in just one paragraph? The opinion "The world should improve" is too broad and general to be discussed adequately in just one paragraph.

Has the writer convinced the reader to agree with his opinion?

Does the writer seem to believe his own point sincerely?

Who was the writer writing for? What did he assume his reader knew about the topic? Was he writing for a specialist, an average reader, or for one totally ignorant of the subject matter?

FOCUS A: SYNTACTIC STRUCTURE

Do the tasks your teacher recommends.

• 1. Task (group or individual)

Jack Agueros wrote about junior high school from the point of view of someone who has left it. Rewrite his paragraph from the point of view of a person in elementary school who is writing about what he believes will be true in the future.

Begin with:

Junior high school <u>will be</u> a waste.

Note: Do not use **will** after **before, after, when, if, until, as soon as.** Use present tense. Underline all the changes you make.

• • 2. Task (individual)

Write one paragraph in which you describe an activity in your life that was "a waste."

Begin with:

_____ was/were a waste.

Examples My music lessons
Reading Shakespeare
Studying history/algebra/geometry/physics
Art lessons

Support that first statement with examples to show how the activity was a waste. Try to convince your reader that your statement is true for you. Use the past tense.

• 3. Task (group or individual)

Are all the sentences in the passage by Agueros complete sentences? Use the **yes/no** question test described in Task 2, pp. 6–7, if you need a checking device. Why do you think Agueros included an incomplete sentence (a sentence fragment)? Did he just not edit carefully, or did he use it for a reason?

Write complete sentences beginning with the words listed below. Remember that a sentence must have an independent subject and predicate that will make a **yes/no** question.

a. When
b. If
c. Although
d. Whenever

e. Because **g.** Even though
f. Since **h.** While

Example Because we had a good teacher. (Fragment)

Because we had a good teacher, English was a good class. (Sentence)

(Was English a good class because we had a good teacher?)

Notice the comma that separates the sentence opener from the base sentence:

Because we had a good teacher, English was a good class.

• 4. Task (individual)

Write five sentences describing five incidents in your life last week. Begin each sentence with the word: **Because.** Remember to use a comma to separate the two sentence parts.

• • 5. Task (individual)

Write out the poem by James Laughlin (p. 79) as prose, adding capitals and punctuation marks.

• • 6. Task (individual)

Write a paragraph with the title of "Obedience in Childhood" or "Disobedience in Childhood." Give examples of the ways in which you and your classmates obeyed or disobeyed school or parental rules.

Vocabulary hints Frequency words: always; often; frequently; occasionally; usually; seldom; rarely; hardly ever; never

Sentence connectors: for example; for instance; that is

• 7. Task (group or individual)

Note the two following sentences:

The math class was permitted **to go** to the gym.
Macy's stopped sell**ing** zip-guns.

Complete the following sentences with:

to + *base form of verb*	**-ing** *form of verb*
The prisoners promised	Most students enjoy
The politicians have decided	A lot of people have stopped
The child refused	They want to give up

to + *base form of verb*	-ing *form of verb*
She didn't expect	The accused man denied
She is planning	The athletes have finished
I want	The dancers kept on
Do you hope	Students often put off

• • **8.** Task (group or individual)

Notice how the parts of the following sentence (by Agueros, p. 82) are joined by **and** and are parallel in structure:

We went from classroom to classroom answer**ing** "here" and try**ing** to be good.

Use the appropriate forms of the sentence parts given below to complete the sentences. Make each item parallel in structure. In some of the sentences you will use all three sentence parts; in others, choose two. The first one is done for you.

Sentence parts:

calculate a square root
describe the causes of the American Revolution
analyze Hamlet's behavior

a. We always tried to avoid _____, _____, and
_____ .

We always tried to avoid calculating a square root, describing the causes of the American Revolution, and analyzing Hamlet's behavior.

b. We always tried to delay _____, _____, and
_____ .

c. We never wanted to _____, _____, or _____ .

d. We soon get tired of _____, _____, and _____ .

e. The whole day consisted of either _____ or _____ .

f. When we arrived at school, we first _____, then _____,
and finally _____ .

g. He failed to graduate not only because he could not _____
but also because he could not _____ .

h. He could neither _____ nor _____ .

i. He never learned how to _____, _____,
or _____ .

j. His friends always enjoyed _____, _____, and
_____ .

• • 9. Task (group or individual)

Read the two paragraphs below.

Whenever an American moves overseas, he suffers from a condition known as "culture shock." Culture shock is simply a removal or distortion* of many of the familiar cues one encounters at home and the substitution for them of other cues which are strange. A good deal of what occurs in the organization and use of space provides important leads as to the specific cues responsible for culture shock.

The Latin house is often built around a patio that is next to the sidewalk but hidden from outsiders behind a wall. It is not easy to describe the degree to which small architectural differences such as this affect outsiders. American Point Four* technicians living in Latin America used to complain that they felt "left out" of things, that they were "shut off." Others kept wondering what was going on "behind those walls." In the United States, on the other hand, propinquity* is the basis of a good many relationships. To us the neighbor is actually quite close. Being a neighbor endows* one with certain rights and privileges, also responsibilities. You can borrow things, including food and drink, but you also have to take your neighbor to the hospital in an emergency. In this regard he has almost as much claim on you as a cousin. For these and other reasons the American tries to pick his neighborhood carefully, because he knows that he is going to be thrown into intimate contact with people. We do not understand why it is that when we live next to people abroad the sharing of adjacent* space does not always conform* to our own pattern. In France and England, for instance, the relations between neighbors are apt to be cooler than in the United States. Mere propinquity does not tie people together. In England neighbor children do not play as they do in our neighborhoods. When they do play, arrangements are sometimes made a month in advance as though they were coming from the other side of town!

EDWARD T. HALL, **The Silent Language**

*Gloss **distortion**   twisted picture
Point Four   program for scientific experts to assist in Latin America
propinquity   nearness
endows   provides
adjacent   neighboring
conform   fit

Discuss with another student which one sentence sums up the opinion the writer is expressing. Write that sentence down. If you think that the topic of the passage is expressed in two or three sentences, write them all down.

Now close your book and, from memory, write down what examples Hall gives to support the topic sentence (s). Use the present tense.

• 10. Task (group or individual)

The following sentences are from the passage about culture shock by Edward T. Hall. Underline the verb phrase in each base sentence and draw a circle around the subject.

Example (He) <u>suffers</u> from a condition known as "culture shock."

a. The Latin house is often built around a patio that is next to the sidewalk.

b. It is not easy to describe the degree to which small architectural differences such as this affect outsiders.

c. In the United States, on the other hand, propinquity is the basis of a good many relationships.

d. To us the neighbor is actually quite close.

e. Being a neighbor endows one with certain rights and privileges.

f. You can borrow things, including food and drink.

g. For these and other reasons the American tries to pick his neighborhood carefully.

h. Mere propinquity does not tie people together.

• • 11. Task (individual)

Culture shock can occur when one visits another country or even a different part of one's own country. (See the passage by Hall, in Task 8 above.) Write down examples of experiences of culture shock, then group these examples together and write a paragraph about culture shock. Make some point about it; Hall talks about the organization and use of space as a cause of culture shock. You could, for example, discuss time, social customs, family organization, social status, gestures, treatment of death, buying and selling, expressing emotions, or eating habits. Concentrate on one area and give examples of situations that cause culture shock. Use the present tense.

• 12. Task (group or individual)

Combine the following groups of sentences. Keep the meaning the same and write only **one** sentence for each group:

a. An American moves overseas.
   He suffers from a condition.
   The condition is known as culture shock.

b. The Latin house is often built around a patio.
   The patio is next to the sidewalk.
   The patio is hidden from outsiders behind a wall.

c. American technicians used to complain.
   They felt "left out" of things.
   They were shut off.

d. You can borrow things.
   They include food and drink.
   You also have to take your neighbor to the hospital in an emergency.

e. The American tries to pick his neighborhood carefully.
   He knows (something).
   He is going to be thrown into contact with people.
   The contact will be intimate.

You can check the passage on p. 87 to see which choices Edward T. Hall made.

FOCUS B: RHETORICAL STRUCTURE

Do the tasks your teacher recommends.

When you make a point, you draw on your own experience and knowledge. But your reader has not been exposed to the same experience and knowledge and needs to know what led you to make your point, whether it was something that happened or something you read. Your reader will not regard you as a reliable source of information if you just throw your point at him and leave—for the next point. He wants to know not only what you think but why you think it. He wants to know why you think your ideas are good. If you just announce, for example, that "Junior high school was a waste," a reader who found his junior high school years productive and exciting would reply with, "But it wasn't for me." He would want to know why you thought it was a waste. If you do not tell him, he will generalize from his own experience and conclude that you are wrong and that your opinions are not worth his time. If you make a statement like "Violence on TV is harmful to children," support it. Show your reader why you think that; what incidents, examples, reading, statistics, personal experience led you to that conclusion? Share your thinking process with your reader.

Consider, too, who your reader is. What you write and the way you write it will change as your audience changes. A description for a friend of your last year at school would be very different from a description for the school principal!

1. Write a paragraph in which you describe your early teenage years, picking out **one** important feature that characterized those years. Were they mainly exciting, boring, miserable, embarrassing? Imagine that you are writing this as part of a formal essay on adolescence. Make sure that the reader can perceive the one dominant feature of those years. Include a topic sentence in your paragraph; this should be the sentence that summarizes the point of your paragraph. Are you going to begin with the topic sentence and then support it? Or are you going to give examples and incidents and then draw a conclusion from them?

    Now rewrite the paragraph as if you were writing informally to a good friend. Keep the same content; just change the language. When you wrote the formal essay, you probably used formal language, with no slang or colloquial expressions. Now your reader has changed, and your writing should change, too.

2. Write an opinion statement about your favorite sport or about a favorite book, movie, or TV show. Is the statement one that you can support with examples to show your reader that you know what you are talking about? If you cannot think of any examples, check that your statement is really an opinion and not a fact (e.g., "TV quiz shows are very popular.") Try again with another statement if you need to. When you have written a statement that you can support with three or four examples, write a paragraph.

3. In a paragraph, make a statement about an outstanding feature of **one** of the following, and give examples to show that feature in action:

    a chameleon   Citizens' Band radio
    litmus paper   educational TV
    a telescope   jazz

4. The situation: You are living in an apartment building with badly insulated walls and floors. You hear a great deal of noise at all hours of the day and night from your upstairs neighbor.

    Write a polite letter to your neighbor complaining about the noise. Give him examples of what kind of noise you hear, and when, and how it disturbs you.

    The situation: It is three months later. The noise has not only continued, but increased. Write a hostile, angry, and threatening letter of complaint to your neighbor. Give examples of the noises you hear and how they disturb you.

    The situation: It is six months later. The noise has continued. Three more people seem to have moved into the apartment above you.

Write a letter to your landlord making the point that you have to break your lease and move out immediately because of the noise. Explain to him your reasons why, clearly and unemotionally. Tell him about some specific occasions on which you have been disturbed by noise.

8

DIVIDING

Focus on these syntactic structures

verbs
> participle form
> present perfect tense
> past tense

verb phrases
> verb + **to** + base form of verb
> verb + **-ing** form of verb

sentence connectors: sequence (**first, next, finally**)

parallel structures

sentence division and punctuation
> commas in a list
> colon before a list

sentence combining

Focus on these rhetorical structures

finding a focus for dividing a topic
dividing a topic into parts

INTRODUCTION

When a flashlight doesn't work any more, before you throw it away it is wise to test if **a.** the batteries are dead, or **b.** the bulb has burned out, or **c.** the switch on the case is not making contact with the batteries. That is, you divide the flashlight into its parts and look at each part in turn. Dividing will help you, too, in writing about any subject that seems very large—especially one that is too large to describe and discuss totally, such as life, the system of justice, art, prejudice, or sports.

CORE COMPOSITION

WHAT I HAVE LIVED FOR

Three passions, simple but overwhelmingly strong, have governed my life: the longing for love, the search for knowledge, and unbearable pity for the suffering of mankind. These passions, like great winds, have blown me hither and thither,* in a wayward course,* over a deep ocean of anguish,* reaching to the very verge* of despair.*

I have sought love, first, because it brings ecstasy*—ecstasy so great that I would often have sacrificed all the rest of life for a few hours of this joy. I have sought it, next, because it relieves loneliness—that terrible loneliness in which one shivering consciousness looks over the rim* of the world into the cold unfathomable* lifeless abyss.* I have sought it, finally, because in the union of love I have seen, in a mystic miniature, the prefiguring vision* of the heaven that saints and poets have imagined. This is what I sought, and though it might seem too good for human life, this is what—at last—I have found.

With equal passion I have sought knowledge. I have wished to understand the hearts of men. I have wished to know why the stars shine. And I have tried to apprehend* the Pythagorean* power by which number holds sway above the flux.* A little of this, but not much, I have achieved.

Love and knowledge, so far as they were possible, led upward toward the heavens. But always pity brought me back to earth. Echoes of cries of pain reverberate* in my heart. Children in famine, victims tortured by oppressors,* helpless old people a hated burden to their sons, and the whole world of loneliness, poverty, and pain make a mockery* of what human life should be. I long to alleviate* the evil, but I cannot, and I too suffer.

This has been my life. I have found it worth living, and would gladly live it again if the chance were offered me.

BERTRAND RUSSELL,
The Autobiography of Bertrand Russell 1872–1914

*Gloss **hither and thither** back and forth, here and there
        wayward course various paths
        anguish pain, agony
        verge edge
        despair loss of hope
        ecstasy great joy, rapture
        rim edge
        unfathomable bottomless
        abyss bottomless hole
        prefiguring vision early glimpse
        apprehend understand
        Pythagorean mathematical (Pythagoras = a Greek mathematician and
          philosopher)
        number holds sway above the flux mathematics is superior to chance
        reverberate echo
        oppressors cruel leaders, tyrants
        mockery false imitation
        alleviate relieve, reduce

1. Bertrand Russell lived until he was 98 years old. His autobiography fills two volumes. Yet here he manages to deal with the complex topic of his life in only five short paragraphs. How has he done that? What is his main idea here (his thesis statement)?

   Individually, write down the thesis statement of the essay (the point of view expressed) and summarize the topic of each of the three middle paragraphs.

Introduction:

Thesis statement:
  I
  II
  III
Conclusion:

2. Exchange papers with another student; read and compare your two summaries.

3. The essay is about Bertrand Russell's life, but obviously he could not cover his whole life in one page. He could, for example, have chosen to focus on his work, his family, his ambitions, or his disappointments. Instead, he chose to focus on the passions that governed his life and then to divide those passions into their parts.

With your partner, discuss the possible divisions of the topic: "Friends I Have Had"

Examples   males   reliable   long hair
               females   unreliable   medium-length hair
                                              short hair

The divisions above have focused on: sex, reliability, and length of hair. How many other divisions can you find? Some other divisions you might focus on are: nationality, age, education, clothes, generosity, length of friendship, politics, life style.

4. Individually, write an essay on **one** of the following topics:

"Friends I Have Had"
"Cities I Have Visited"
"Classes I Have Attended"
"Games I Have Played"
"Parties I Have Been To"

Choose a definite focus for your division of the topic into parts. Write four to seven paragraphs (an introduction, a conclusion, and middle paragraphs for the divisions of your topic). Before you begin to write your essay, ask yourself these questions:

Questions   How am I going to look at this topic—what will be the focus of my division?

How many divisions can I make?

Do my divisions cover the topic completely? (For example, a division of "students" into " 'A' students" and " 'F' students" is not complete. What about all the rest?)

Do I have examples, incidents or facts for each of my divisions?

Which part of my division will I discuss first? Last? What is the most logical order? (Look at Russell's essay again. Why do you think he chose the order of: love, knowledge, pity, instead of the other way around?)

OCUS A: SYNTACTIC STRUCTURE

Do the tasks your teacher recommends.

• 1. Task (individual)

In the essay by Bertrand Russell on p. 93, underline all the verb phrases with

has
have   + **participle** (present perfect tense)

95

Examples have governed   have sought

Now give the base form of the verbs you have listed:

govern   seek

Now underline any present perfect tense verbs you used in the essay you wrote for the Core Composition of this chapter. Check to make sure that you did not mention any definite past time with any of those verb forms. (There should be **no** expressions like: last week, last year, a few weeks ago, when I was little, in 1970).

• 2. Task (group or individual)

Fill in the necessary verbs and auxiliaries in the essay by H. L. Mencken below. Notice the verb tense he uses: the present perfect tense. Does he ever tell us exactly when any of the events happened? Or do we just know that they happened some time during the eight-and-a-third years that he had been editing and writing for the magazine **The American Mercury?** The piece below is from his one-hundredth column for the monthly magazine.

TAKING STOCK

All in all, [it was] a harsh and forbidding life, and yet, after eight and a third years, I still pursue it and if all goes well I hope to print my thousandth article in February, 1991. In those eight and a third years I have _____ (serve) four editors, not including myself; I have _____ (grow) two beards and _____ (shave) them off; I have _____ (eat) 3,086 meals; I have _____ (make) more than $100,000 in wages, fees, refreshers,* tips and bribes; I have _____ (write) 510,000 words about books and not about books; I have _____ (receive), _____ (look at), and _____ (throw away) nearly 3,000 novels; I have _____ _____ (call) a fraud 700 times, and have _____ (blush) at the proofs; I have _____ (have) more than 200 invitations to lecture before women's clubs, Chautauquas,* Y.M.C.A.'s, chambers of commerce, Christian Endeavor societies, and lodges of the Elks; I have _____ (receive) 150 pounds of letters of sweet flattery; I have myself _____ (write) and _____ (publish) eight books, and _____ (review) them all favorably; I have _____ (have) seventeen proposals of marriage from lady poets; I have _____ _____ (indict)* by grand juries eight times; I have _____ (discover) thirty bogus* geniuses; I have _____ (be) abroad three and a half times, and have _____ (learn) and _____ (forget) six foreign languages; I have _____ (attend) 62 weddings, and have _____ (spend) nearly $200 for wedding presents; I have _____ (gain) 48 pounds in weight and _____ (lose) 18 pounds, and have _____ (grow) bald and gray; I have _____ _____ (convert) by the Rev. Dr. Billy Sunday, and then _____ (recant)* and _____ (go) back to the devil; I have _____ (wear out) nine suits of clothes; I have narrowly _____ (escape) marriage four times; I have _____ (have) lumbago and neuralgia; I have _____ (take to)* horn-rimmed spectacles; I have _____ (elude)* the white-slave traders; I have _____ (fall) downstairs twice; I have _____ (undergo) nine surgical operations; I have _____ (read) the **Police Gazette** in the barbershop every week; I have _____ (shake) hands with Dr. Wilson; I have _____ (uphold) the banner of the ideal; I have _____ (keep) the faith, in so far as I could make out what it was; I have _____ (love) and _____ (lie); I have _____ (get) old and sentimental; I have _____ _____ (torpedo)* without warning.

H.L. MENCKEN, March 1917, **Smart Set Criticism**

*Gloss **refreshers**   extra fees
Chautauquas, etc.   all of these are clubs
indict   accuse, charge with a crime
bogus   fake, not real
recant   take back a statement, change mind
take to   adopt, begin using
elude   avoid
torpedo   bomb under water

The complete version is in the Appendix on p. 174.

• • 3. Task (individual)

Write a one-paragraph account of the past five years of your life. Do not mention exact dates or times of events. List, as Mencken did (Task 2, above), the things that you **have done** during that time. Use the present perfect tense throughout.

Example I have moved five times.

• 4. Task (group or individual)

Imagine that H. L. Mencken had written his essay "Taking Stock" (p. 174) after he was no longer writing for the **American Mercury.** All the events would now be related to a definite past time. Rewrite the passage, using the **past tense.**

Begin with:

When I used to work for the **American Mercury,** I <u>served</u> four editors. . . .

Underline all the changes you make.

• • 5. Task (individual)

Write thirteen sentences about things that you have **often** or **always** done. Use all the verbs below, in the present perfect tense (**have** + **participle**), followed by appropriate verb phrases:

verb + to + *base form of verb*	*verb* + -ing
try	avoid
want	enjoy
hope	finish
fail	resent
expect	dislike
plan	give up
intend	

Examples I **have** always **disliked** getting bad grades.
I **have** always **wanted to do** well in school.

• • 6. Task (individual)

Notice the repetition of the following structure in Bertrand Russell's essay (p. 93):

I have sought . . . because. . . .

Notice also the use of the sentence connectors:

first . . . next . . . finally. . . .

Imagine that you are 75 years old. Write an essay with four to six paragraphs with the title: "What I Have Lived For." To unify your essay, use some sentence connectors and some repeated parallel structures.

• 7. Task (group or individual)

Notice the parallel structures in the two sentences from the passage by Mencken (p. 96):

I have made more than $100,000 in **wages, refreshers, tips,** and **bribes.**

I have **received, looked at,** and **thrown away** nearly 3,000 novels.

Complete the following sentences with parallel structures, separated by commas:

a. For breakfast this morning, I had _____, _____, and _____.

b. I have never _____, _____, or _____.

c. Her three ambitions are to _____, to _____, and to _____.

d. Most children enjoy _____, _____, and _____.

e. Yesterday was a bad day for her; all day long she felt _____, _____, and _____.

• 8. Task (group or individual)

Examine all the uses of the word **and** in the passage by Mencken on p. 96. Write down each sentence, and write on separate lines any parallel structures that are joined by **and.**

Examples I have loved
> **and**
> lied.

I have been called a fraud 700 times
> **and**
> have blushed at the proofs.

Leave out any sentences that have more than one **and** in them.

• • 9. Task (individual)

In the first sentence of Bertrand Russell's essay on p. 93, the colon (:) is used before a list:

Three passions have governed my life: the longing for love, the search for knowledge, and unbearable pity for the suffering of mankind.

Here the colon means "and these three passions are." Write six sentences of your own consisting of a base sentence, a colon, and a list.

Examples I bought some summer clothes last week: sandals, a light shirt, and shorts.

I invited four friends to join me on the picnic: Marie, Rosa, Eva, and Lisa.

• 10. Task (group or individual)

Combine the following groups of sentences. Keep the meaning the same and write only **one** sentence for each group.

a. I have grown two beards.
   I have shaved them off.

b. I have received nearly 3,000 novels.
   I have looked at nearly 3,000 novels.
   I have thrown away nearly 3,000 novels.

c. I have attended 62 weddings.
   I have spent nearly $200 for wedding presents.

d. I have been abroad three times.
   I have learned six foreign languages.
   I have forgotten six foreign languages.

e. I have loved.
   I have lied.

f. I have gotten old.
   I have gotten sentimental.

You can check p. 174 to see which choices Mencken made.

FOCUS B: RHETORICAL STRUCTURE

Do the tasks your teacher recommends.

A good way to look at an object, an institution, or an idea is to divide it up into its basic parts. A high school, for example, consists of teachers, students, administrators, and staff members. An egg consists of yolk, white, and shell. An argument consists of reasons for it and reasons against it. Dividing a topic gives you a clear framework for organizing your writing.

Dividing can be used, too, to sort objects or people into groups. You could organize an essay about students, for example, by dividing them into two groups: full-time students and part-time students. Or you could divide them into three groups: those who spend a lot of time in the library, those who spend some time in the library, and those who spend no time in the library. The groups you choose will be determined by what you want to say about your topic: do you want to discuss the benefits of full-time study, or do you want to discuss students' study habits?

1. Empty out the contents of a pocket, a handbag, a briefcase, or a drawer. One way to tell someone about the objects would be to describe them in random order. Another way would be to divide the contents into groups. Make a list of the objects and then try two or three different ways of grouping them. Give each of your groups a label. For example, if you

group objects according to **color,** your labels might then be **red, yellow,** and **blue.** Consider also grouping according to size, shape, material, and use.

2. With a group of students, choose **one** word from the following list:

   eyes   cars   food   hair   transportation   footwear

   What comes into your mind when you hear that word? Give spontaneous one-word reactions. For example:

   eyes   brown   love   Maria   cry   blue

   Write down all the words your group produces. If you now had to write an essay on that topic, you could use your random list of words as your raw material. Divide the words into groups. Leave out any which do not fit into a group. Give each group of words a label. For example, on the topic of "eyes," one group of words might be:

   emotions   cry   tears   tired   smiling

3. Read the passage from Mencken's "Taking Stock" on p. 174. He gives a random list of activities. Can you find any way to group the activities he mentions and then to split the essay up into paragraphs? Make an outline of the paragraphs you would make and the details you would include in each paragraph.

Example   I. Personal appearance
    A. beards
    B. weight
    C. spectacles
  II.
    A.
    B.
    C.

4. The broad topics below can be narrowed by dividing them into parts or types. Find a clear focus for division and make sure that all the parts or types are included in your division. Choose **one** of the topics and write an essay of four to seven paragraphs. The division you choose should help you to express an opinion about the topic.

Example   Topic: drivers
Focus: speed
Divisions: slow drivers   speed-limit drivers   speeders

Opinion: Slow drivers are as dangerous as fast drivers.

Topics   teachers   movies   music   advertising   anxiety   superstition
a typical teenager

9

COMPARING AND CONTRASTING

Focus on these syntactic structures

    modifiers
        comparative forms (**than; (not) as . . . as**)
        superlative forms
    sentence connectors
        similarity (**and so . . .; both . . . and; also**)
        contrast (**but, however, in contrast,** etc.)
    pronouns and pronoun reference
    verbs
        past tense
        participle form
    sentence division: subject and predicate
    agreement: singular/plural
    word forms: adjective, noun, verb, adverb
    verb phrases
        verb + **to** + base form of verb
        verb + **-ing** form of verb
    sentence combining

Focus on these rhetorical structures

    finding points of comparison
    organizing a comparison and contrast essay: two models
    making an outline

INTRODUCTION

Comparing and contrasting is something that you all do every day. You pick up two apples, look at them, and decide which one to eat. You pause outside two department stores, and decide to shop in one. You are offered two jobs, and decide to take one. Before you decide, you compare and contrast the details in your head. You look for the points that are similar (comparing) and the points that are different (contrasting). Sometimes, when an important decision like choosing a job has to be made, you might even write down lists of the similarities and differences to help you decide. Writing an essay of comparison and contrast is just an extension of this logical thought process.

CORE COMPOSITION

THE DIVISION OF LABOR BY SEX IN THE MEXICAN VILLAGE OF TEPOZTLÁN

The division of labor according to sexes is clearly delineated.* Men are expected to support their families by doing all the work in the fields; by caring for the cattle, horses, oxen, and mules; by making charcoal and cutting wood; and by carrying on all the large transactions* in buying and selling. In addition, most of the specialized occupations, such as carpentry, masonry, and shoemaking, are done by men. An important function of the father of the family is to train his sons in the work of men. When a Tepoztecan* man is at home, his activities consist of providing* the household with wood and water, making or repairing furniture or work tools, making repairs on the house, and picking fruit. Men also shell corn when shelling has to be done on a large scale.* Politics and local government, as well as the organization and management of religious and secular fiestas,* are also in the hands of the men.

Women's work centers about the care of the family and the house. They cook, clean, wash, iron clothes, do the daily marketing, shell the corn for daily consumption,* and care for the children. Mothers train their daughters in women's work and supervise* them closely until their marriage. Many women raise chickens, turkeys, and pigs; and some grow fruit, vegetables, and flowers to supplement* the family income. Women do a great deal of buying and selling on a small scale, and they control the family purse. Tepoztecan women are not expected to work in the fields, and Tepoztecans of both sexes look down upon the women of the neighboring villages who do agricultural work, carry heavy loads of firewood or corn on tump lines,* wear men's hats, and generally appear rougher and coarser* than do the women of Tepoztlán.

OSCAR LEWIS, **Life in a Mexican Village**

*Gloss **delineated** defined
transactions business deals
Tepoztecan from the village of Tepoztlán
providing . . . with giving
shelling . . . large scale removing a lot of husks
secular fiestas non-religious festivals, celebrations
consumption eating
supervise watch over
supplement add to
tump lines straps across the head to support bundles carried on the back
coarser harsher, more vulgar

1. Examine the paragraph structure in Oscar Lewis's account of the division of labor in the Mexican village of Tepoztlán. What is the topic of each paragraph? What examples are given? Complete the following paragraph outline:

    I. Topic: What men do
       Examples:
       A. work in the fields
       B. look after the animals
       C.

    II. Topic:
        Examples:
        A.
        B.
        C.

2. When you have finished your list of examples for both paragraphs, examine them to see if they can be divided into groups with titles, such as: agriculture, work in the home. Which examples from paragraph I and from paragraph II are similar in topic?

3. With a partner, make an outline for a four to five paragraph essay comparing men's jobs and women's jobs in Tepoztlán. The topics of the paragraphs will now be the main types of jobs done. Use only the information Lewis gives.

Example I. Topic: Child care
       Examples:
       A. Men: train sons
       B. Women: train daughters and look after young children

II. Topic:
Examples:
A.
B.

III. Topic:
Examples:
A.
B.

If some of Lewis's examples do not fit into your new division, leave them out.

4. Make two lists of the jobs women do and the jobs men do in a family or village that you know well. Write one paragraph describing the jobs women do, and another describing the jobs men do. Are the jobs clearly defined?

Begin with:

In _____ (my family; a Chinese village; etc.), the division of labor according to sexes is (not) clearly delineated.

5. Reorganize the examples in your two lists, so that you can write three to four paragraphs. The topic of each paragraph will now be the type of job (for example: cooking, cleaning the house, repairing equipment, earning money) and in each one you will compare and contrast what women do and what men do.

6. Compare your two essays and write down answers to the following questions:

Questions From each essay, can you make a clear outline, as you did in Tasks 1 and 3, above? Make the outlines.

Have you included all the points you listed in each of your essays? If not, what was your reason for omitting them?

Have you used any phrases that compare or contrast?

Examples **Compare** **Contrast**

Compare	Contrast
similarly	in contrast (to)
likewise	on the other hand
as . . . as	not as . . . as
also	but
too	however
as well as	nevertheless

If you have not, would your essays point out the comparison and contrast more clearly if you added some?

FOCUS A: SYNTACTIC STRUCTURE

• • 1. Task (group or individual)

Rewrite the sentences below using the given words and phrases. Keep the meaning the same.

Example   Swimming is **as** healthy **as** running.
use **and so**: <u>Swimming is healthy and so is running.</u>

    a. Swimming exercises many muscles **and so** does running.
        Use **both . . . and** _____

    b. Swimming is good for you **and** running is **too.**
        Use **both . . . and** _____

    c. Swimming is **as** good for you **as** running is.
        Use **and . . . too** _____

    d. **Both** swimming **and** running improve your stamina.
        Use **and so** _____

    e. Swimming is **more** strenuous **than** table-tennis.
        Use **less . . . than** _____

    f. Table-tennis is not **as** energetic **as** swimming.
        Use **more . . . than** _____

    g. Table-tennis is **less** beneficial **than** swimming.
        Use **not as . . . as** _____

Which of the above sentences show similarity and which show contrast?

• 2. Task (group or individual)

Complete the following sentences of contrast:

    a. Compared to boys, girls _____ .

    b. Girls are more _____ than boys.

    c. Boys _____ but girls do not.

    d. Boys _____ but girls are not.

    e. In contrast to boys, girls are _____ .

    f. Girls _____ . Boys, on the other hand, _____ .

    g. Boys _____ . Girls, however, _____ .

    h. Girls _____ , while boys _____ .

• **3.** Task (group or individual)

Read the following paragraph:

The significant aspect of the American scene is that there is a discrepancy* between the way **we** bring up boys and girls—each to choose both a job and a marriage partner—and then stylize* housekeeping as a price the girl pays without stylizing the job as the price the boy pays. Men are trained to want a job in a mill, or a mine, on a farm, in an office, on a newspaper, or on a ship as a sign of **their** maleness, **their** success, and to want a wife and children to crown that success; but women today are not given the same clear career-line—to want an apartment, or a semi-detached house, or a farm-house, or a walk-up,* or some other kind of home, as **their** job. The American woman wants a husband, yes, children, yes, a home of **her** own—yes indeed, it's intolerable to live with other people! But housekeeping—**she** isn't sure she wouldn't rather "do something" after **she** gets married. A great proportion of men would like a different job—to have at least better pay, or higher status, or different working conditions—but **they** are not asked to face the seeming discrepancy between being reared* for a choice and reared to think that success matters, and also that love matters and that everyone should marry, and yet not be able to feel that the mate one chooses and the job one does after marriage are independent. It is as if a man were to make a set of plans for **his** life—to be an accountant, or a lawyer, or a pilot—and then have to add, "Unless of course, I marry." "Why?" **you** ask. "Because then **I'll** have to be a farmer. **It's** better for the children, **you** know."

MARGARET MEAD, **Male and Female,** 1949

*Gloss **discrepancy**   disagreement
stylize   characterize, represent
walk-up   an apartment in a building with no elevator
reared   raised, brought up

Examine the pronouns in bold type in Margaret Mead's paragraph. List them, and next to each one, write down what or whom it refers to. If the referent is mentioned in the text, give the exact word(s) of the text.

Example **their** maleness = men

• **4.** Task (group or individual)

Margaret Mead wrote her book **Male and Female** in 1949. Rewrite the paragraph from it in Task 3, above, in the past tense.

Begin with:

Margaret Mead said that the significant aspect of the American scene in 1949 <u>was</u> that there <u>was</u> a discrepancy. . . .

Underline all the changes you make. (Do not change Mead's direct speech at the end.) Change **today** to **in those days.**

• 5. Task (group or individual)

Rewrite Lewis's account of the division of labor in Tepoztlán on p. 103 as if you were a historian looking back on what the village was once like. You will use the past tense.
　Begin with:

The division of labor according to sexes <u>was</u> clearly delineated. Underline all the changes you make.

• 6. Task (group or individual)

In Lewis's account of the division of labor in a Mexican village (p. 103), underline any of the following verb sequences:

$$\left.\begin{array}{c} \text{be} \\ \text{am / is / are} \\ \text{was / were} \\ \text{being} \\ \text{been} \end{array}\right\} + \text{participle}$$

Example　　　is　　　　　delineated

Write down the sentence in which each one occurs, and circle its subject.

Example　(The division of labor according to sexes)　is clearly <u>delineated</u>.

• 7. Task (group or individual)

Rewrite the second paragraph of Lewis's account (on page 103) changing **women** to **a woman.** (Change **many women** to **one woman;** change **some** to **another.**) Underline all the changes you make.
　Begin with:

<u>A woman</u>'s work centers about the care of the family and the house.

• **8.** Task (group or individual)

Imagine you are a copywriter for an advertising agency. You are writing an advertisement to promote **one** of the following:

Grinno, a new toothpaste
Puffo, a new cigarette
Staingo, a new detergent
Munchies, a new breakfast cereal

Write six sentences comparing the new product to other brands and praising its superlative qualities.

Examples	Comparative:	Grinno is **more** effective **than** Shyno.
		Grinno tastes bet**ter than** Shyno does.
		Grinno is **as** tingling fresh **as** Shyno is.
	Superlative:	Grinno cleans **the** whit**est** of all.
		Grinno is **the most** effective toothpaste in the world.

• • **9.** Task (individual)

Go to the Reference Room of a library and browse through the **Guinness Book of World Records.** Make notes on the main ideas in three of the entries that interest you the most. Twenty-four hours later, without looking at your notes, write as much as you can remember about the three entries you read and summarized. Underline any superlative forms you have used: the most; the fastest, etc.

• • **10.** Task (group or individual)

In the following passage, fill in the appropriate form of the given word. Use a dictionary if necessary.

Most [researchers] have settled on stress and what they call "Type-A" behavior as the prime* candidates for _____ (psychology) causes of heart attacks. A person who shows Type-A behavior is _____ (high) _____ (compete), feels pressured for time, and reacts to _____ (frustrate) with _____ (hostile). My research focuses on the interplay between the Type-A personality, life stress, and heart attack.

In order to _____ (classification) people as Type A or Type B, I use their _____ (respond) to questions about their _____ (ambitious), _____ (competitive), sense of being pressed for time,* and _____ (hostility) feelings. Type-A people, for example, are likely to set deadlines or quotas* for themselves at work or at home at least once per week, while Type-B people do so only _____ (occasion). A Type-A person brings his work home with him _____ (frequent), a Type-B almost never. The Type-A person is highly achievement-oriented,* and pushes himself to near capacity, while the Type-B person takes it easy. Hard-driving Type-A students earn more _____ (academically) honors than their Type-B counterparts, though they are no more _____ (intelligence). The Type-A behavior pattern earns a person the reward he seeks, but at a cost to his body that may be the _____ (dead) of him. Obviously, not all Type-A people have heart attacks, but there are certain times, especially when they come under severe stress, when their risk of heart attack is greatest.

DAVID C. GLASS, "Stress, Competition, and Heart Attacks"

*Gloss **prime**   main
pressed for time   short of time
quotas   limits
achievement-oriented   directed toward being successful

The complete original version is on p. 175.

• 11. Task (group or individual)

Circle the pronouns in the passage from the article on "Stress, Competition, and Heart Attacks," on p. 175. See the pronoun chart on p. 21 for a listing of pronoun forms. Draw a line from each word that you circle to connect it to the word(s) the pronoun refers to.

Example Type-A people, for example, are likely to set deadlines or quotas for themselves at work or at home at least once per week.

• • 12. Task (individual)

Read the passage from the article "Stress, Competition, and Heart Attacks" on p. 175. Then close this book and write six sentences comparing the two types—Type A and Type B.

Vocabulary hints more . . . than; -er than; (not) as . . . as; but; however; on the other hand; in contrast; compared to; while

Examples Type A is more competitive than Type B.
Type B is not as interested in achievement as Type A is.

•• 13. Task (group or individual)

Look at the following list of adjectives:

aggressive ambitious competitive restless impatient
self-confident decisive resolute punctual obsessive hostile

They can be used in sentence slots like:

He is an **aggressive** man.
She is **aggressive**.
Many **aggressive** people have heart attacks.

Give the **noun form** of the above adjectives, so that the word will fit into a sentence slot like:

Type A is characterized by **aggression**.
He acts with **aggression**.
Aggression is a feature of his personality.

Use a dictionary if you need help.

•• 14. Task (individual)

Notice the following verb phrases:

Men avoid tak**ing** care of small children.
(*verb* + ——ing *form of verb*)

Men are expected **to** support their families.
(*verb* + to + *base form of verb*)

Use these forms to write sentences that compare or contrast male and female students. Use as many as you can of the following verb phrases:

verb + to + *base form of verb*		*verb* + ——ing *form of verb*	
expect	plan	enjoy	postpone
decide	want	resent	insist on
hope	intend	dislike	avoid

Examples Most boys dislike study**ing** at night and girls do too.
                                  and so do girls.
                                  but girls do not.

Girls don't want **to take** every course and neither do boys.
                                  and boys don't either.

•• 15. Task (group or individual)

Write a paragraph comparing and contrasting **either** cats and dogs as household pets, **or** movies and television as exciting entertainment, **or** buses and trains as efficient means of transportation. Limit your comparison to the given topic. Do not compare every aspect of the pair you choose. For example, discuss how movies and TV are **entertaining,** not how they are educational.

Vocabulary hints but; however; nevertheless; in contrast; in comparison; on the other hand; more . . . than; less . . . than; equally; just as

• 16. Task (group or individual)

Combine the following groups of sentences. Keep the meaning the same and write **one** sentence only for each group.

a. Type A is ambitious.
Type B is easygoing.

b. Type A works hard all the time.
Type B enjoys leisure.

c. Type A is competitive.
Type B is not competitive.

d. It is hard to make Type B angry.
It is not hard to make Type A angry.

e. Type A goes to bed early.
Type B does not go to bed early.

f. Type A always becomes impatient.
Type B seldom becomes impatient.

FOCUS B: RHETORICAL STRUCTURE

Do the tasks your teacher recommends.

Comparing and contrasting are common thought processes that you use every day: which coat to wear, which movie you recommend, which person you like best. In writing, you can compare and contrast several different subjects with each other, or you can divide one topic into parts and then compare and contrast the parts. You can, for example, compare two cars. Or you can divide "students" into groups and compare and contrast these groups. The processes of comparison and contrast might even help you to form an opinion about the subject—which car is better, or which group of students will find better jobs.

Whenever you compare and contrast when you write, your first task is to ask **how** you are going to organize your material, and here you have two structures to use as models. Let's say that you are comparing two people,

A and B. You decide on four points of comparison—1, 2, 3, and 4, which might be looks, personality, ambitions, and work habits. You can take the **whole** approach and organize like this:

Person A	**Person B**
Point 1	Point 1
Point 2	Point 2
Point 3	Point 3
Point 4	Point 4

Or you can, with a little more work on your part, take the **point** approach and organize the same material like this:

Point 1	**Point 3**
Person A	Person A
Person B	Person B
Point 2	**Point 4**
Person A	Person A
Person B	Person B

This second organization saves the reader some work; he doesn't have to refer back to work out how A differs from B in relation to point 3. The writer has done that job for him. Whichever form of comparison you decide to use, make sure that you are comparing things that can logically be compared: socialism and communism, yes; but socialism and tennis, no.

1. Write a three to four paragraph essay in which you compare and contrast some aspects of the behavior of male and female students.

    How will you organize your essay? Will you discuss men's behavior in one paragraph and women's behavior in another? Or will you discuss an aspect of behavior, such as "the scheduling of time" and compare and contrast how men and women schedule their time? Try out both types of organization in a rough outline form before you begin to write the essay. Show your teacher your outlines before you begin to write.

2. Compare and contrast the personality of two of your friends or two members of your family. Use the **point** approach and choose three or four points on which to compare the people.

3. Compare and contrast city living with country living. Reach some conclusion about which you prefer and give your reasons why.

4. Would you classify yourself as a Type-A or a Type-B person according to Glass's division (p. 175)? Compare and contrast yourself to those two types, referring to the characteristics that are discussed in Glass's article. Give examples of your own behavior to support your points.

5. Divide people into two or three types and compare and contrast the types. Express an opinion about the types.

Examples people who have children / people who do not have children
people who enjoy food / people who do not enjoy food
young / middle-aged / old

6. Using the **point** approach, compare and contrast **one** of the following pairs. Examine one point of comparison in each paragraph. Use detailed examples for each of the objects being compared.

two schools
two restaurants
two cars
two scientific methods
two poems

7. Use the library resources to gather information on **one** of the following pairs of topics, and then write an essay of about 150–200 words comparing and contrasting the two topics:

a red cell and a white cell
a termite and an ant
a bee and a wasp
soul music and country western music
an economic recession and a depression
the ego and the id
Democrats and Republicans
an ode and a sonnet
judo and karate
basketball and volleyball
socialism and communism
sociology and anthropology
psychology and psychiatry

10

EXPLAINING A PROCESS

Focus on these syntactic structures

    verbs
        passive/active
        present and past tenses
        participle form
        base form
    sentence division and punctuation
    modifiers: **-ing** and **-ed**
    sentence connectors
        sequence (**first, next, then,** etc.)
        addition (**also, in addition,** etc.)
    pronouns and pronoun reference
    sentence combining

Focus on these rhetorical structures

    writing explanations: chronological order
    linking the steps

INTRODUCTION

You explain a process whenever you give someone directions to the post office. If your directions are not clear, if you leave out an important step (like forgetting to tell the person whether to turn left or right along Main Street), or if you do not describe the steps in the right order, then your listener might end up at the fish market instead of the post office.

You yourself use written explanations of a process whenever you follow a recipe, a diet, or an exercise routine. You also follow instructions when you assemble a child's toy, paint a room, or operate a washing machine. So you probably know from experience how important it is for explanations to be clear and well-organized.

CORE COMPOSITION

1. With a group of students, choose **one** of the following topics; discuss what steps are involved in the process, and in what order.

   how to make bread (spaghetti) (ice cream)
   how to make a paper airplane
   how to roll a cigarette
   how to change a fuse
   how to put up a tent
   how to dissect a frog
   how to make a bed

   Individually, write a paragraph explaining the process, step by step.

Vocabulary hints Words to connect sentences to show time sequence: first; next; then; finally; meanwhile; in the meantime; afterwards; subsequently

Words to connect sentences to add ideas: in addition; also; furthermore; too; moreover

Words to combine sentences to show time relationships: after; before; while; when; as soon as; until

Example Before you attempt anything, you must first turn the electricity off.

2. Read the following passage:

HOW ENZYMES ARE STUDIED

In order to study this enzyme,* a small piece of potato is cut into very thin slices. These slices are placed in a little glass container and covered with water. Then a little of the proper chemical is added. Instantly, because of the enzyme present in the potato slices, the chemical starts combining with the oxygen in the air above the water. If the container is entirely closed, a partial vacuum* is formed inside. If the container is now connected with a fine tube which is dipped in water, the water is sucked* part way up the tube because of the vacuum. (The principle is the same as that by which we suck soda up a straw.)

The scientist conducting the experiment carefully notes how far up the tube the water is sucked in a certain time. The higher it is sucked, the more of that particular enzyme is in the potato. In this way, we can obtain* quite accurate* notions* about quantities of enzyme and even about the manner in which it operates. And all the time we're working with amounts far too small to see or weigh.

ISAAC ASIMOV, **The Chemicals of Life**

*Gloss **enzyme**   an organic substance in plants and animals
vacuum   space with no air
sucked   pulled
obtain   get
accurate   exact
notions   ideas

Discuss with your group how this passage would be different if it was called: "How To Study Enzymes." Discuss also the difference between sentences like these two:

The proper chemical is added.
We suck soda up a straw.

In which one is the subject of the sentence **active** (doing the action) and in which one is the subject of the sentence **passive** (having something done)? Who did the **adding?** Who did the **sucking?**

3. Write a second paragraph on the same topic that you chose for Task 1, but this time write it with the emphasis on the process and on the object. The topics will now be:

how bread (spaghetti) (ice cream) is made
how a paper airplane is made
how a cigarette is rolled
how a fuse is changed
how a tent is put up
how a frog is dissected
how a bed is made

You will not be giving your reader instructions. You will be telling him what is usually done in this process.

Example Before anything is attempted, the electricity must first be turned off.

4. Give your two paragraphs to another student and read that student's two paragraphs. As you read them, think about and write down answers to the questions below. Then discuss your answers with your partner.

Questions How many steps are there in the process described?

Are they all included, and in the same order, in both paragraphs?

What words are used to link steps in the sequence?

Are the steps in the sequence in chronological order?

Is the process clear to you? Could **you** follow the instructions without having to ask any additional questions?

For what kind of reader and occasion would the first paragraph (with **active** verbs) be written, and for what kind of reader and occasion would the second paragraph (with **passive** verbs) be written?

FOCUS A: SYNTACTIC STRUCTURE

Do the tasks your teacher recommends.

• 1. Task (group or individual)

Rewrite the passage by Asimov on p. 116 as if it were called not "How Enzymes Are Studied" but "How To Study Enzymes."
  Begin with:

In order to study this enzyme, cut a small piece of potato into very thin slices.

Use **active** rather than passive verb forms wherever possible. Be careful when you get to the part about water being sucked up the tube: who or what is doing the sucking?

• • 2. Task (group or individual)

Read the following passage:

HOW THE TARZAN YELL WAS MADE

M-G-M* spared no expense on the Tarzan yell. Miles of sound track of human, animal and instrument sounds were tested in collecting the ingredients of an unearthly howl. The cry of a mother camel robbed of her young was used until still more mournful sounds were found. A combination of five different sound tracks is used today for the Tarzan yell. These are: 1. Sound track of Weissmuller* yelling amplified.* 2. Track of hyena* howl, run backward and volume diminished.* 3. Soprano note sung by Lorraine Bridges, recorded on sound track at reduced speed; then rerecorded at varying speeds to give a "flutter" in sound. 4. Growl of dog, recorded very faintly. 5. Raspy* note of violin G-string, recorded very faintly. In the experimental stage the five sound tracks were played over five different loud speakers. From time to time the speed of each sound track was varied and the volume amplified or diminished. When the orchestration* of the yell was perfected, the five loudspeakers were played simultaneously and the blended* sounds recorded on the master sound track. By constant practice Weissmuller is now able to let loose an almost perfect imitation of the sound track.

*Gloss **M-G-M**   Metro Goldwyn Mayer, a movie production company
Weissmuller   Johnny Weissmuller, who played Tarzan in the M-G-M movies
amplified   made louder
hyena   dog-like animal with a shrill, laugh-like cry
diminished   reduced
raspy   rough
orchestration   arrangement
blended   mixed

The list of the five different sound tracks, numbered 1 through 5, is composed of sentence fragments; each one is completed by the introductory "These are:" which begins the list. (Compare this with the introductory "There we saw:" of the essay by John Updike on p. 42).

Rewrite each of these fragments as complete sentences, telling what was done to produce the yell. Just omit the phrase "These are:" and add any necessary verbs and articles to change each fragment into a sentence. Use the present tense to write about **today.**
   Begin with:

A combination of five different sound tracks is used today for the Tarzan yell. The sound track of Weissmuller yelling is amplified. . . .

(§2) • 3. Task (group or individual)

Rewrite the new paragraph you wrote for Task 2, above, in the **past** tense, as if you were a historian recording how the Tarzan yell was made many years ago.

Begin with:

A combination of five different sound tracks <u>was</u> used for the Tarzan yell. The sound track of Weissmuller yelling <u>was</u> amplified. . . .

Underline all the changes you make.

• • 4. Task (group or individual)

Discuss with other students the question of who is or was doing each of the actions in the passage about Tarzan on p. 118.

Miles of sound track were tested . . .
by whom?

A mother camel was robbed of her young . . .
by whom?

The sound track of Weissmuller yelling is amplified . . .
by whom?

Is it important for us to know? Does the writer think it is important for us to know?

Rewrite the whole passage, emphasizing the M-G-M engineers and all the things **they did** to produce the yell. You will change **passive** verbs to **active.**

Begin with:

M-G-M spared no expense on the Tarzan yell. The M-G-M engineers tested miles of sound track. . . .

Omit the phrase "These are:" before the list, and write each item in the list as a complete sentence, again using **they** or the **engineers** as the subject of the sentence.

Example The engineers amplified the sound track of Weissmuller yelling. They . . .

• 5. Task (group or individual)

In the passage about enzymes on p. 116 underline all the **participle** forms of verbs that have been used to form the **passive** voice. Here is a test you can make: if the idea of "**by** someone or something" can be added, that is a passive verb.

Example My room is <u>cleaned</u> every week. (by someone)

• 6. Task (group or individual)

Rewrite the passage about enzymes on p. 116 as if you were a historian of science in the year 2500 describing a procedure used by scientists many years ago. Use the **past** tense.

Begin with:

In order to study this enzyme, a small piece of potato <u>was</u> cut into very thin slices.

Change **we** to **they.** Underline all the changes you make.

• 7. Task (individual)

Examine the **-ing** and **-ed** verb forms used in the various adjective slots in the sentences below:

His rude remarks were **embarrassing.**

It was **embarrassing** when he made those rude remarks.

He made a lot of **embarrassing** remarks.

The **embarrassed** guests left. (They were **embarrassed** by his remarks.)

She felt **embarrassed** by his rude remarks.

She left because she was very **embarrassed.** (by his remarks)

Write sentences using both **-ing** and **-ed** adjective forms of the verbs in the list below:

frighten   shock   amaze   surprise   interest   confuse   bore
disappoint

• • 8. Task (group or individual)

Make an alphabetical listing of words ending in **-ed** to fit into this sentence:

A student feels **ashamed** when he . . .
                bored

Continue with the letters **c, d,** etc. Use a dictionary if necessary. If you get stuck at any letter, like **k** or **x,** move on to the next one.

• 9. Task (group or individual)

Divide the words and phrases listed below into two groups:

a. Words that can begin a report, letter, or composition; and
b. Words that cannot begin a report, letter, or composition.

finally   for example   perhaps   usually   however   afterwards
in addition   first of all   moreover   nevertheless   in general
in my opinion   on the other hand

•• **10.** Task (group or individual)

Put the given word into the second sentence of the pair so that it connects
the ideas of the two sentences. Write sentences showing all the possible
positions in the sentences for those connecting words.

a. Stephen is an architect. He is a painter. (also)

b. Michael is a sculptor. He is a carpenter. (too)

c. Peggy directs a movie company. She writes film scripts. (in addition)

d. Paul has designed a cabin, children's beds, and theater scenery. He has designed his own huge circular shower. (moreover)

e. All four of them are innovative artists. They are good friends. (furthermore)

• **11.** Task (group or individual)

Add capital letters and punctuation to the following recipe:

GINGER SNAPS

assemble the following ingredients 4 ounces of butter 4 table-
spoons of syrup 2 teaspoons of ground ginger 1 teaspoon of grated
lemon rind 3 ounces of flour and 3 ounces of sugar now put the
butter the sugar the lemon rind and the syrup into a pan and melt
over low heat meanwhile sift the flour and the ginger together and
then mix them into the melted ingredients drop a teaspoonful at a
time on to a well-greased cookie sheet bake in a slow oven (300°)
for about 10 minutes as the ginger snaps are cooling pick them up
and roll them into tubes fill each one with whipped cream

• **12.** Task (individual)

In the second paragraph (passive) you wrote for the Core Composition of
this chapter, circle all the pronouns you used. (For a chart of pronouns,
see Task 3, p. 21.) Draw a line connecting each pronoun to the word or
words it refers to.

Example The paper is folded in half lengthwise and then (it) is folded again on each side.

•• 13. Task (group or individual)

Write one sentence using each of the following verb phrases; add appropriate expressions of time.

was building	was built
has fixed	has been fixed
has been stealing	has been stolen
is writing	is written
is considering	is being considered
will be taking	will be taken
will move	will be moved
should be planning	should be planned

Example She was building a bookcase all last week.
That bookcase was built by a thirteen-year-old girl.

• 14. Task (group or individual)

Pretend you are a witch. Give instructions on how to prepare a monstrous witch's brew to serve as a meal to your enemies. Use sentence connectors to link the steps in the process (see p. 116). Use the base form of verbs.

Example **Find** five large slimy toads and . . .

(§14) • 15. Task (group or individual)

Rewrite the instructions you wrote for Task 14, telling a friend what **was done** without mentioning who did it. You will be giving information on how the brew **was made.** Your reader will not be told who made it. Use the past tense (passive).

Example Five large slimy toads **were found** and . . .

• 16. Task (group or individual)

Combine the following groups of sentences. Keep the meaning the same and write only **one** sentence for each group.

a. These slices are placed in a container.
The container is made of glass.
The container is little.
The slices are covered with water.

b. The container is now connected with a fine tube.
The tube is dipped in water.

c. The cry of a mother camel was used.
The mother camel was robbed of her young.

d. The orchestration of the yell was perfected.
The five loudspeakers were played simultaneously.
The blended sounds were recorded on the master sound track.

e. The water has boiled.
Add the spaghetti.

f. The spaghetti is hard.
You will need to wait.
The part in the water will get soft.

g. The spaghetti is cooked.
Eat it.

FOCUS B: RHETORICAL STRUCTURE

Do the tasks your teacher recommends.

Explaining a process involves giving a reader instructions on how to do something or giving a reader information on how something is or was done. Instructions and information, like all other types of expository writing, need clear organization. Have you ever tried to follow directions for assembling a toy or a piece of equipment and run into difficulty because the instructions have been incomplete or not in sequence? You have probably, at some time or another, turned the page of a recipe and found, "Add the sliced mushrooms." **What** sliced mushrooms? How many? They haven't been mentioned before—and there you are with the dish half made and not a mushroom in the house. Or you have been assembling a piece of equipment only to find, in the last stages, that the part that holds it all together is a Phillips screw—and of course you have no Phillips screwdriver.

When you explain a process, remember to describe the equipment and the steps in detail and in order. With this type of writing especially, you must know exactly who you are writing for: are your readers totally ignorant of the topic, or are they familiar with the topic and its terminology? In explaining, for instance, how to give mouth-to-mouth resuscitation, you will write at one level for the general public and another for hospital personnel who are familiar with medical terminology. You don't want a patient to die because his Aunt Rosa doesn't know what his sternum is.

1. Write instructions for someone to prepare your favorite cooked dish. Plan first how you will organize your instructions: will you just move step by step, or will you begin by explaining what ingredients have to be assembled beforehand?

Add a paragraph, either at the beginning or at the end, in which you say why you like this dish so much.

2. Write an explanation of how you wrote any one recent assignment from this book. Give details: where were you, did you make a draft, use a type-writer, did you interrupt the writing process, what equipment did you use?

3. Write an explanation of how you were raised during early childhood. Use chronological order, with details of people, places and attitudes that were expressed toward you. Use both active and passive forms. Use active forms when you are interested in stating **who** did the action.

4. Write a step-by-step detailed explanation of **one** of the following topics. Use library resources if you need to collect information.

how tadpoles develop into frogs
how caterpillars change into butterflies
how an octopus mates
how bees make honey
how birds build nests
how food is digested
how cars are mass-produced

5. Write an explanation of a technical procedure that you know very well, for example:

how to start a car on a cold day
how to measure blood pressure
how to operate a telephone switchboard
how to assemble a transistor radio
how to change a tire

Write the explanation first for a reader who is familiar with the topic and with the general procedure, but just needs to be reminded. This reader will be familiar with technical terminology.

Then rewrite your explanation for a different reader—this time for a complete layman, a novice who knows nothing at all about the topic and is not familiar with its technical language.

11

DEFINING

Focus on these syntactic structures

> clauses: **who, which, that, where**
> word forms
> **-ing** phrases
> agreement: singular/plural (with **who, which,** etc.)
> pronouns and pronoun reference
> sentence combining

Focus on these rhetorical structures

> defining a concrete object
> defining a concept
> using denotation and connotation

INTRODUCTION

In discussions, misunderstandings sometimes occur because people do not agree on the definition of the term they are discussing. For example, if two students are discussing how to be successful in their later life, they might find after a while that for one of them earning a lot of money means success, while for the other, having happy family relationships means success. Obviously, any discussion of how to be "successful" must here begin with definitions of "success." Otherwise there will be no real discussion, but just two separate speeches. In writing, your reader is not there to ask you, "What exactly do you mean by 'success'?" so you have to anticipate this question, and define the term in advance.

CORE COMPOSITION

SHAME

A tendency among grownups is to sentimentalize* childhood. They concentrate on its playfulness, its innocence and its freedom from responsibility. But the fact is that the process of growing up involves experiencing emotions that often are painful. Indeed, in childhood we learn how to cope* with the complexities* of those feelings that define us as human beings. One emotion that is particularly intense in childhood is shame. The feeling of shame is inevitable to a self still in formation, and even the most normal child can attest* to its pain.

The dictionary has varied definitions for the word "shame." Synonyms* range from "embarrassment" to "mortification" to "humiliation." The experience of shame is described as a loss of pride* or self-respect—a sense of being ridiculous, indecent or unworthy.* Here is the way one child talks about such a moment:

"I tried to cook my own breakfast and I dropped the pan on the floor and I burned a hole in the tile and Mommy woke up and yelled at me and said I could never turn on the stove again." As she speaks her voice is ragged;* her eyes are averted;* her self-confidence obviously is submerged under a burning sense of failure.

In his theories on identity, psychoanalyst Erik Erikson, widely regarded as a major authority on children, links the feeling of shame with that of self-doubt. The child too often shamed at her failed attempts to stand on her own feet* can begin to doubt that she ever will be able to take that position in life. One of the great dilemmas* of growing up is how to leave childhood's natural helplessness without taking along all those feelings of inadequacy* that were felt as a child.

No matter how rapidly a child grows physically, secret feelings of shameful smallness, weakness and incompetence often pulsate* inside. To the child, these characteristics are to be hidden at all costs, for in the child's mind they translate as "stupid," "silly," "babyish," and the idea of exposure* is a dreadful threat. So intense is the fear of exposure that in his anxiety* the child may dream of running naked along school halls, unable to find a hiding place, looking down while reciting in class to find that his pants have fallen to the floor or going to a party and finding he is wearing the wrong clothes. Asleep or awake, he has a sense of being pinned down and revealed under the harsh light of a judging "other" while derisive* laughter swells* louder and louder around his flaming* ears.

Not surprisingly, then, in talking about being ashamed, children fall into particular patterns of creative expression. "It's like your skin is all ripped off your body," says Robert, his face flushed with emotion. "It's like your skin is peeled away in big pieces and you gotta cry and cry and cry, like Mommy would if she peeled a million onions. . . ."

Then Andy, who has reflected for a moment on Robert's analogy,* adds his own clearly similar conception.* "Being ashamed is like your head is cut open by a big piece of metal like I saw in that sheet-metal factory we went to with the class . . . and the whole inside of your head is all hanging out. . . ."

CAROLE KLEIN, **The Myth of the Happy Child**

Title supplied. A.R.

*Gloss **sentimentalize** be emotional about
cope manage
complexities difficulties
attest give proof
synonyms words with the same meaning
pride sense of one's value
unworthy not deserving respect
ragged uneven, rough
averted turned away
stand on her own feet be self-reliant
dilemmas problems
inadequacy failing, inability to deal with a situation
pulsate beat
exposure display
anxiety worry
derisive scornful
swells grows

flaming hot and red
analogy comparison
conception idea

1. With other students, write definitions of the following terms to explain them to someone (perhaps a child) who does not know what they are:

   a rose   a sentence   honesty

   Which one was the hardest to define? Why? Now look up each of the words in the dictionary.

2. Here are the dictionary definitions of the word **shame:**

   shame (shām), n. [<AS. scamu], 1, a painful feeling of guilt, indecency, etc. 2. dishonor; disgrace. 3. something unfortunate or outrageous. v.t. [SHAMED, SHAMING], 1. to cause to feel shame. 2. to dishonor; disgrace. 3. to force by a sense of shame. **—put to shame,** 1. to cause to feel shame. 2. to surpass. **—shaméful,** adj.

   With permission. From **Webster's New World Dictionary**, Popular Library, Pocket-Size Edition. Copyright © by The World Publishing Co.

   All dictionaries contain a guide to the abbreviations and symbols used. With other students, work out what the abbreviations and symbols used above mean.

3. Sometimes words mean different things to different people. The dictionary definition (the denotation) is then not enough; you need to add the meanings that the word has for you (connotations). Read the passage about "Shame." Carole Klein quotes some dictionary definitions and then adds the definition made by a famous psychoanalyst. In addition, she makes her own idea of **shame** even clearer to the reader by giving examples from children's own experience: one child describes an incident when she experienced the feeling of shame, others compare the feeling to other feelings and experiences.

   With other students, discuss and make a list of some other examples that you might add to this definition.

4. The word **home** is one that might have many different meanings (connotations) for many different people living in different places and in different centuries. With your group, discuss how **you** would define the term **home.** What is **home**? Does it have the same meaning for all the students in the group? After discussion, write down a list of your definitions. Then look up the word **home** in the dictionary. Compare your connotations with these from Robert Frost's poem "The Death of the Hired Man":

   'Home is the place where, when you have to go there,
     They have to take you in.'
                                   'I should have called it
   Something you somehow haven't to deserve'.

5. Individually, write a paragraph defining **home.** Make use of a dictionary definition and synonyms, and your own incidents, examples, information, and comparisons.

6. Exchange papers with another student. Notice how this student's definition is different from yours. Write down answers to the following questions about the student's paragraph:

Questions   Which dictionary definition does the writer give?

Has the writer put quotation marks around any exact quotations?

What examples has the writer given of a personal definition of **home?**

Has the writer narrated any incidents?

Do you know now exactly what the writer means by the term **home?** How is his definition similar to or different from yours?

FOCUS A: SYNTACTIC STRUCTURE

Do the tasks your teacher recommends.

• 1. Task (group or individual)

Define the following concrete objects so that someone who has never seen or heard of them will know what they are. Try to avoid using the word **thing** in your definitions.

a wrench   a blender   flip-top cans   a pocket calculator
a zipper   a Phillips screwdriver

Vocabulary   tool; container; device; instrument;
hints   which; that

• • 2. Task (group or individual)

Give definitions of what the following people are. If necessary, use a dictionary to help you.

gynecologist   plumber   lexicographer   philatelist   pediatrician
accountant   carpenter   sculptor   psychiatrist   lawyer

Example   A(n) _____ is _____ who _____
A cardiologist is a doctor ⎫ who treats heart disease.
                someone ⎭

• • 3. Task (group or individual)

While everyone might agree on what a wrench is, not everyone would agree on what **fear** or **loneliness** are. Discuss with other students possible definitions for these concepts:

loneliness   fear   prejudice   luxury   jealousy

Notice the structures:

Fear is anxiety.
Fear is the feeling which (that) you get when . . .
Fear is hearing a noise in your room at night.

Write a short paragraph of definition for **one** of the terms in the list above.

• 4. Task (group)

The novel **Love Story** by Erich Segal ends with "Love means never having to say you're sorry." With five or six other students, write **one** one-sentence definition of love each, beginning "Love means . . ." Write these definitions one below the other, arranged to read like a poem.

• • 5. Task (group or individual)

Write definitions of the following, in answer to the question: "What is?"

an atheist   an ascetic   a parsnip   a volcano   a motel   a resort
a vampire   a cynic   a concerto   a kangaroo   a termite
a hurricane

Vocabulary hints   To refer to people: who (that)
To refer to animals: which; that
To refer to things: which; that
To refer to places: where

Example   A polyglot is a person } who speaks a lot of languages.
                                someone }

(§5) • 6. Task (group or individual)

Rewrite the sentences you wrote for Task 5 above, using plural forms.

Example   Polyglots <u>are people</u> who <u>speak</u> a lot of languages.

Underline all the changes you make.

131

• • **7.** Task (group or individual)

Define six of the following processes:

medical	**culinary**	**legal**
X-ray	simmering	indictment
cauterization	frying	impeachment
vaccination	roasting	probation
natural childbirth	poaching	bail

Example Vaccination is a medical process **in which** . . .
by which . . .

• **8.** Task (group or individual)

In paragraphs 2, 3, and 4 of the article about "Shame" on p. 127, find all the pronoun forms. (See Task 3, p. 21 for a pronoun chart.) Make a list of the sentences with pronouns used in these three paragraphs, and next to each one write the exact word or words in the text that the pronoun refers to. Underline the pronoun forms.

Example As <u>she</u> speaks, <u>her</u> voice is ragged.—one child

• • **9.** Task (group or individual)

The following words in the chart are taken from the first paragraph of the article about shame by Carole Klein on p. 127. Write the corresponding word forms in the blanks below. Use a dictionary if necessary. Leave out word forms in blanks marked with #.

Example successful   success   succeed   successfully

Adjective	**Noun**	**Verb**	**Adverb**
#	tendency	_____	#
_____	_____	sentimentalize	_____
#	_____	concentrate	#
_____	playfulness	_____	_____
_____	innocence	#	_____
_____	freedom	_____	_____
#	responsibility	#	_____
#	process	_____	#
_____	_____	involve	#
painful	emotion	#	_____
_____	_____	_____	_____
_____	complexity	#	#
_____	_____	define	_____
_____	#	#	particularly

intense	_____	#	_____
_____	shame	_____	_____
inevitable	_____	#	_____
_____	formation	_____	#
normal	_____	#	_____

• 10. Task (group or individual)

Give the noun forms of the verbs below. Use a dictionary if necessary.

decide   expect   reject   separate   realize   investigate   solve
admire   contribute   demolish

Example	verb	noun
	suggest	suggestion

• • 11. Task (group or individual)

In the given sentences from Margaret Mead's essay "On Friendship," fill in the appropriate form of the word in parentheses at the end of the sentence.

a. No one really expects a vacation trip to _____ a close friend. (production)

b. But surely the beginning of a friendship is _____? (possibility)

c. Surely in every country people _____ friendship? (valuable)

d. The difficulty when strangers from two countries meet is not a lack of _____ of friendship. (appreciate)

e. In those European countries that Americans are most likely to visit, friendship is quite _____ distinguished from other, more casual relations. (sharp)

f. Friendship is _____ related to family life. (difference)

g. For a Frenchman, a German or an Englishman friendship carries a heavier burden of _____. (commit)

h. But as we use the word, "friend" can be _____ to a wide range of relationships. (application)

i. There are real _____ among these relations for Americans. (different)

j. A friendship may be superficial, casual, situational or _____ and enduring. (deeply)

The passage the sentences were taken from is on p. 176 in the Appendix.

• **12.** Task (group or individual)

Combine the following groups of sentences. Keep the meaning the same, and write only **one** sentence for each group.

a. With each move we are forever making new friends.
They become part of our new life at that time.

b. Today millions of Americans vacation abroad.
They go to see new sights.
They go with the hope of meeting new people.

c. To a European the differences between "friendships" are not clear.
The European sees only our surface behavior.

d. People flow in and out of Americans' homes.
The people are known.
The people are accepted temporarily.
The people are accepted casually.

e. The European visitor comes as a guest into an American home.
The European visitor finds no visible landmarks.

You can check on p. 176 to see which choices Margaret Mead made.

FOCUS B: RHETORICAL STRUCTURE

Do the tasks your teacher recommends.

How often have you argued with a friend, reached a dead end, and then realized that you did not agree on the meanings of the terms you were using? How often have you said, "Ah, yes, but it depends what you mean by . . ."? The point you want to make depends on your meaning being clear. Before communication can be effective, you and your reader have to have common ground for the definitions of words. Read the following discussion:

"I don't know what you mean by 'glory' " Alice said.

Humpty Dumpty smiled contemptuously.* "Of course you don't —till I tell you. I mean 'there's a nice knock-down argument for you!' "

"But 'glory' doesn't mean 'a nice knock-down argument,' " Alice objected.

"When I use a word," said Humpty Dumpty, in rather a scornful tone, "it means just what I choose it to mean, neither more nor less."

"The question is," said Alice, "whether you **can** make words mean so many different things."

"The question is," said Humpty Dumpty, "which is to be master —that's all."

LEWIS CARROLL, **Through the Looking Glass**

*Gloss contemptuously   scornfully

But **you** cannot, like Humpty Dumpty, take "glory" to mean "there's a nice knock-down argument for you" just because you feel like it. If you do, your reader will not only not understand but will think that the writer (you!) has gone crazy.

If you are writing about a subject that involves an unfamiliar term (a "quark," for example), that term must be defined. Familiar but broad terms like "democracy" should be defined, too, if your reader is to find out which meaning (s) the concept has for you. When you give your definition of a concept—"civilization" or "success" for example—use examples, incidents, division, and comparison and contrast to show what meaning(s) the term has for you. If you don't, your reader will use his own personal definition, which might be very different from yours.

1. Choose **one** of the following topics:

intelligence   success   masculinity   femininity   megalomania
paranoia   reincarnation   behaviorism   filibuster   ascetism

Define it in an essay. In addition, give examples of it, compare and contrast it to another term, or divide it into parts. Your essay should have about five or six paragraphs. Use dictionaries, encyclopedias, magazine and newspaper articles, and books to help you gather information. In your essay you should express an opinion you hold about the topic, and support it.

2. Read the following definitions of **a friend**:

A friend is a person with whom I may be sincere.
Before him, I may think aloud.
RALPH WALDO EMERSON, **Essays: First Series,** 1841

A friend is one soul abiding in two bodies.
DIOGENES LAERTIUS, **On Aristotle,** A.D. 200

One friend in a lifetime is much; two are many; three are hardly possible. Friendship needs a certain parallelism of life, a community of thought, a rivalry of aim.
HENRY ADAMS, **The Education of Henry Adams,** 1907

Write your own extended definition, with examples, of **a friend**.

3. E. B. White wrote a short humorous poem defining a commuter:

Commuter—one who spends his life
In riding to and from his wife.
A man who shaves and takes a train
And then rides back to shave again.

E. B. WHITE, from The Lady Is Cold

Write a short poem describing **one** of the following:

a dog owner   an elevator operator   a professional tennis player
a drummer   a chef   an obstetrician   a dentist   a dietician
a teacher   an office clerk

4. A passage from an article on boredom states:

Boredom is a grossly underestimated malady.* It causes mischief
and destruction; it is socially very expensive. Erich Fromm identi-
fies it as the insidious* cause of catastrophes* ranging from drug
addiction to violence. Bertrand Russell said that "boredom is a
vital problem for the moralist since at least half the sins of mankind
are caused by fear of it."

ESTELLE R. RAMEY,
"Boredom: The Most Prevalent American Disease"

*__Gloss__ **malady**   disease
insidious   treacherous and dangerous
catastrophes   disasters

In an essay, define boredom, and discuss the causes and results of
boredom.

12

REPORTING

Focus on these syntactic structures

> direct quotation and punctuation
> reported speech
>> tense sequence
>> pronouns
>> word order
> included questions
> sentence division and punctuation
> capitals
> sentence combining

Focus on these rhetorical structures

> using and acknowledging sources
> quoting
> paraphrasing

INTRODUCTION

I asked her if she could do me a favor.

She said I shouldn't have left so early.

He asked me to work late on Friday.

He shouted, "And they're off!" every time the train started moving.

We often use sentences like those above to tell people what we and others said. Reporting is a frequent part of everyday conversation. Telling a reader what another writer said is frequent in writing, too. It shows your reader that you are an informed writer who knows what others have said about the topic.

CORE COMPOSITION

© 1968 United Feature Syndicate, Inc.

1. With some other students, write an account of the conversation between Charlie Brown and Lucy in the cartoon.

Begin with:

One day Lucy was sitting . . .

Use the exact words of the conversation in direct speech, with quotation marks.

Example With a gloomy expression on his face, Charlie Brown said, "I'm lonely."

Notice that the following passage includes direct speech. Refer to it if you need help with the punctuation of writing direct speech.

> Lee crossed his legs. He stared at his shoes and frowned.
> "**What's the matter?**" I asked.
> "**Do you know something?**" Lee said. "**I've been wearing this pair of shoes ever since I came to New York. The same shoes every day for three months.**"
> "**Don't you have any others?**" Daphne asked.
> "**That's not the point,**" he said. "**The thing is that they aren't beginning to wear out. Why, my God, when I was in school I used to walk through a pair of shoes in a month. Do you think that is a sign of something?**"
> Daphne didn't know.
> "**Well,**" Lee said, "**I'm not going to pursue the thought. I might get a complex.**"
>
> AUBREY GOODMAN, **The Golden Youth of Lee Prince**

2. Compare the paragraph your group wrote with a paragraph written by another group. Examine the punctuation.

3. Still with your group, rewrite your first paragraph without using quotation marks or first person pronouns like **I** or **we**.

   Begin in the same way:

   One day Lucy was sitting. . . .

   Notice that you have two statements, a question, a command, and a request. What introductory verbs will you use other than **said**? What verb tense will you use throughout? What happens to the question (and the question mark) when it is included in a statement?

Example With a gloomy expression on his face, Charlie Brown told Lucy that he was lonely.

4. Still in your group, write down answers to the following questions:

Questions What changes did you have to make when you wrote reported speech?

Which of your two versions do you like better? Why?

Which one seems to be more formal in tone? Why?

What verbs did you use to introduce the speech? Did you use anything other than **said** or **asked**? Alternatives would be: **stated, complained, muttered, whispered, replied, responded, inquired, exclaimed.**

In what kind of writing do you usually find direct speech?

In which of the following would you usually find reported speech: minutes of meetings; newspaper reports; academic essays; literary criticism; novels; comic strips; sociological surveys?

If you were recounting a conversation a long time later and could not remember the exact words used, would you use direct quotations, or reported speech?

5. Individually, write a paragraph in which you give an account of a short interesting conversation between two people that you know. Use direct quotation, with quotation marks.

FOCUS A: SYNTACTIC STRUCTURE

Do the tasks your teacher recommends.

• • 1. Task (group or individual)

Rewrite the passage from **The Golden Youth of Lee Prince** on p. 139 using reported speech (**no** quotation marks). You will have to change or leave out any expressions that belong specifically to speech, such as "my God" or "Well."

• • 2. Task (individual)

Rewrite the account you wrote of a conversation between two people (Task 5 of the Core Composition). This time use reported speech and no quotation marks. Use the past tense throughout.

• 3. Task (group or individual)

In the Core Composition of Chapter 5 (p. 57), there are eight questions. The first one is:

What did he look like?

Rewrite those questions as questions included in a sentence beginning with **I don't know.**

Example I don't know what he looked like.

• 4. Task (group or individual)

In the Core Composition of Chapter 5 (p. 58), there is a list of included questions (questions included in a sentence). The first one is:

how often the phone rang

Rewrite these included questions as direct questions, with a question mark at the end.

Example How often did the phone ring?

• • 5. Task (individual)

In March 1973, **The New York Times** reported how, at a party, "an argument over who was to get the last piece of chicken to eat ended when one man stabbed another to death." Write an account of the conversation at the party that led up to the stabbing. Give names to the people involved. Use **direct** quotation.

(§5) • 6. Task (individual)

Rewrite your account of the party conversation in Task 5 using reported speech with **no** direct quotation.

• • 7. Task (individual)

Reread the interview with Truman Capote in Chapter 4, p. 44. Close the book and paraphrase (i.e., tell entirely in your own words) what was discussed in the interview.
Begin with:

The interviewer began by asking Capote about his writing habits. Capote told him that. . . .

Use the past tense throughout.

• • 8. Task (individual)

Reread Oscar Lewis's account about the division of labor in Tepoztlán (p. 103). Close the book and make a list of the most important points Lewis made. Write a paragraph paraphrasing (stating in your own words) the points made by Lewis. Include only **one** direct quotation from Lewis—of a sentence or part of a sentence that you consider particularly significant. Use the quotation to illustrate one of Lewis's points that you mention in your paraphrase.

• 9. Task (group or individual)

Add punctuation and capital letters to the following passage from Ray Bradbury's science fiction story "November 2005: The Luggage Store."

"We don't hear the explosions."

we will   said the proprietor   I keep thinking about all those
people that were going to come to mars this week   what was
it   a hundred thousand or so coming up in the next month or so
what about them if the war starts

I imagine they'll turn back   they'll be needed on earth

well   said the proprietor   I'd better get my luggage dusted
off   I got a feeling there'll be a rush sale here any time

do you think everyone now on mars will go back to earth if this
is the big war we've all been expecting for years

it's a funny thing   father   but yes   I think we'll all go back

The complete text is on p. 145. Check your punctuation with the author's.

• 10. Task (group)

Write three questions that you would like to ask another student, beginning with:

Do?   What?   When?

Example Do you live with your parents?

The student you ask will refuse to answer. Now write three sentences
including the unanswered question in each sentence after **I don't know.**

Example I don't know if (name of student) lives with his/her parents.

• 11. Task (group or individual)

Combine the following groups of sentences. Keep the meaning the same
and write only **one** sentence for each group. Use reported speech.

   a. He said (something).
     He wanted to leave early.
     This surprised everybody.

   b. I wonder (something).
     "What time is it?"

   c. I don't know (something).
     "Where does he live?"

   d. I don't know (something).
     "Where has he gone?"

   e. I wanted to know (something).
     "Where has he gone?"

f. I asked him (something).
"Where do you work?"

g. I asked her (something).
"Do you have time to help me?"

OCUS B: RHETORICAL STRUCTURE

Do the tasks your teacher recommends.

You report what someone said or wrote in everyday conversation, in letters, in reports, and in academic essays. A great deal of academic writing refers to other sources as authorities and summarizes the main points of what someone else wrote. Using other people's ideas and opinions to back up your own makes your argument stronger and lets your reader see that you have consulted informed sources who agree with your point of view. Refuting other people's ideas also shows that you have been thorough in your research and have considered opinions that are different from your own. Don't just bombard your reader with someone else's words and ideas. Use what others have said to support what **you** think.

You don't have to include huge chunks of direct quotation to prove that you have done your research. Summarize other writers' views in your own words, and use direct quotation to add a vivid touch, to emphasize a particularly significant idea, or to provide an effective conclusion.

1. Read a newspaper article or a magazine article that interests you. Write a report of what the article says. Use your own words, with no direct quotation from the original article. Attach the article to your report.

2. Go to the Reference Room of a library and read about a subject that interests you in an encyclopedia. Read the encyclopedia article twice, then close the book and write a paraphrase of what you read. Begin by acknowledging where you found the information:

   According to the **Encyclopaedia Brittanica,**[1] the main feature of jazz is that it is improvised.

   In a footnote at the bottom of the page, give the title of the entry, and the year of publication. You do not need to repeat the name of the encyclopedia, as you have already mentioned it.
   Sample footnote:

   [1] "Jazz," 1974.

3. In the Reference Room of a library, read a dictionary of biography or any other reference book for information about the life of **one** of the following:

Shirley Chisholm	Charlie Parker
Harriet Beecher Stowe	Stanford White
Madame Curie	Gertrude Stein
W. C. Fields	Emily Dickinson

In your own words, with the book closed, summarize the information you find. Acknowledge your source in a footnote; your total information (in the text and the footnote) should include:

the title of the entry (in a dictionary) or the name of the author
the name of the reference book (underlined)
the place of publication and the publisher
the year of publication
the volume number (in roman numerals) if more than one volume
the page number

Your reader then knows exactly where to look if he wants more information. If you use any of the wording of the original passage, you must put it into quotation marks.

Sample quotation and footnote:

When Harriet Beecher Stowe was young, she read a great deal of romantic fiction and spent time in "morbid introspection."[2]

[2] James D. Hart, **The Oxford Companion to American Literature**, 4th ed. (New York: Oxford University Press, 1965), p. 812.

4. Read the following science fiction story by Ray Bradbury. Summarize the plot in your own words: report what happens and what the characters say to each other. Use reported speech.

NOVEMBER 2005:
THE LUGGAGE STORE

It was a very remote* thing, when the luggage-store proprietor* heard the news on the night radio, received all the way from Earth on a light-sound beam. The proprietor felt how remote it was.

There was going to be a war on Earth.

He went out to peer into the sky.

Yes, there it was. Earth, in the evening heavens, following the sun into the hills. The words on the radio and that green star were one and the same.

"I don't believe it," said the proprietor.

"It's because you're not there," said Father Peregrine, who had stopped by to pass the time of evening.

"What do you mean, Father?"

"It's like when I was a boy," said Father Peregrine. "We heard about wars in China. But we never believed them. It was too far away. And there were too many people dying. It was impossible.

Even when we saw the motion pictures we didn't believe it. Well, that's how it is now. Earth is China. It's so far away it's unbelievable. It's not here. You can't touch it. You can't even see it. All you see is a green light. Two billion people living on that light? Unbelievable! War? We don't hear the explosions."

"We will," said the proprietor. "I keep thinking about all those people that were going to come to Mars this week. What was it? A hundred thousand or so coming up in the next month or so. What about **them** if the war starts?"

"I imagine they'll turn back. They'll be needed on Earth."

"Well," said the proprietor, "I'd better get my luggage dusted off. I got* a feeling there'll be a rush sale here any time."

"Do you think everyone now on Mars will go back to Earth if this **is** the Big War we've all been expecting for years?"

"It's a funny thing, Father, but yes, I think we'll **all** go back. I know, we came up here to get away from things—politics, the atom bomb, war, pressure groups, prejudice, laws—I know. But it's still home there. You wait and see. When the first bomb drops on America the people up here'll start thinking. They haven't been here long enough. A couple years is all. If they'd been here forty years, it'd be different, but they got relatives down there, and their home towns. Me, I can't believe in Earth any more; I can't imagine it much. But I'm old. I don't count. I might stay on here."

"I doubt it."

"Yes, I guess you're right."

They stood on the porch watching the stars. Finally Father Peregrine pulled some money from his pocket and handed it to the proprietor. "Come to think of it, you'd better give me a new valise.* My old one's in pretty bad condition. . . ."

RAY BRADBURY, **The Martian Chronicles**

*Gloss **remote** far away
proprietor owner
got have (conversational)
valise suitcase

13

SPECULATING

Focus on these syntactic structures

> verbs
>> conditions (**if** . . .)
>> modal verbs (**could, might,** etc.)
>> future tense
>> base form
> sentence combining

Focus on these rhetorical structures

> speculating about past, present, or future
> formulating a hypothesis

INTRODUCTION

It is not only fortune tellers who speculate about the future. Every time you use words like **probably, possibly, maybe, might,** or **if,** you are speculating. In writing, it is quite likely that you will present a point of view based on a hypothesis. You might, for example, argue that if man's pollution of the natural environment continues, man will kill himself. You have to use your imagination when you speculate, but you also need facts and examples to show that your speculations are reasonable. You can't just announce that "Man will be extinct by the year 2005" without giving some basis for the speculation.

CORE COMPOSITION

BABOON CHASED 3 HOURS AT A MARYLAND AIRPORT

An escaped 65-pound baboon led pursuers* on a three-hour, slapstick* chase through Friendship International Airport today but was caught when he ducked* into a ladies room.

The baboon charged around the airport complex, leaping over chairs and counters and running along corridors. Citizens scurried* as the police, state troopers, and terminal employees chased the animal.

The baboon escaped from his cage in the airport freight area where he was awaiting delivery from New York to Johns Hopkins Hospital for a research project. In the ladies room where he was cornered,* he was put to sleep with a shot from a tranquilizing* gun. A spokesman for the airport police described him as "docile* but very, very quick."

The New York Times, October 4, 1973

*Gloss **pursuers** people chasing
slapstick comedy based on accidents such as falling down, bumping into things, and dropping things
ducked ran suddenly
scurried ran away fast
cornered trapped in a corner
tranquilizing calming
docile easy to manage

1. Read the article from **The New York Times** about the escaped baboon. This one was captured quickly, but a baboon on the loose for a long time at a large airport could cause unlimited chaos. In pairs or groups, discuss the possibilities of what **might have happened** if the baboon had not been caught so fast. Make a list of possible events.

2. Individually, write a paragraph for a newspaper column. Head the paragraph:

Capture of Baboon Prevents Airport Chaos

Begin by summarizing what actually happened at the airport and then speculate about the possible results of a longer dash for freedom. What **could have/might have** happened? Use your imagination to develop a good story.

3. Exchange papers with another student. Write answers to the following questions about the other student's account.

Questions Has the writer written down his speculations in random order, or in the order in which they might have actually happened, or in climactic order (leading up to the most important point)?

Which order would be the most appropriate for a newspaper account?

Has the writer speculated about any one event that might be more extreme, more disastrous, more amusing than the others? If so, where did he mention it in his account? First, in the middle, or last?

FOCUS A: SYNTACTIC STRUCTURE

Do the tasks your teacher recommends.

• 1. Task (group or individual)

Make a list of superstitions. Use an **if** clause, and the future tense.

Example If you break a mirror, you **will** have seven years of bad luck.

• 2. Task (individual)

In a story by Dorothy Parker called "The Standard of Living," two girls play a game of asking each other, "What would you do if you had a million dollars?" There is one condition: you must spend all the million dollars on yourself. Write two or three paragraphs discussing what you would do or buy for yourself. Notice the verb forms here compared to the verb forms in Task 1 above. What is the difference in the speaker's attitude in these two sentences?

If you **break** a mirror, you **will** have seven years of bad luck.
If you **broke** a mirror, you **would** have seven years of bad luck.

Compare also the following sentences. Which one would an optimist say?

If I **win** the lottery, I **will** give you $5,000.
If I **won** the lottery, I **would** give you $5,000.

• • 3. Task (individual)

Write a paragraph with the title:

How My Life Might Have Been Different

Use structures like:

If I **had gone** to a different school, I **would have** learned more.

Notice the verb forms:

would have
If I **had** (+ participle gone) . . . , I could have (+ participle learned) more.
might have

• • 4. Task (group or individual)

Read the following passage:

There are whole libraries of books about the Thirties and millions of feet of films, still and moving. It is a completely recorded and documented period. But to those who lived through the period and perhaps were formed by it, the Thirties are a library of personal memories. My own recollections will not be exactly like others, but perhaps they will set you thinking and raise up your memories.

The Depression was no financial shock to me. I didn't have any money to lose, but in common with millions I did dislike hunger and cold. I had two assets.* My father owned a tiny three-room cottage in Pacific Grove in California, and he let me live in it without rent. That was the first safety. Pacific Grove is on the sea. That was the second. People in inland cities or in the closed and shuttered industrial cemeteries had greater problems than I. Given the sea a man must be very stupid to starve. That great reservoir of food is always available. I took a large part of my protein food from the ocean. Firewood to keep warm floated on the beach daily, needing only handsaw and ax. A small garden of black soil came with the cottage. In northern California you can raise vegetables of some kind all year long. I never peeled a potato without planting the skins. Kale, lettuce, chard, turnips, carrots and onions rotated* in the little garden. In the tide pools of the bay, mussels were available and crabs and abalones* and that shiny kelp* called sea lettuce. With a line and pole, blue cod, rock cod, perch, sea trout, sculpin* could be caught.

I must drop the "I" for "we" now, for there was a fairly large group of us poor kids, all living alike. We pooled our troubles, our money when we had some, our inventiveness,* and our pleasures. I remember it as a warm and friendly time. Only illness frightened us. You have to have money to be sick—or did then. And dentistry also was out of the question, with the result that my teeth went badly to pieces. Without dough* you couldn't have a tooth filled.

It seems odd now to say that we rarely had a job. There just weren't any jobs. One girl of our group had a job in the Women's Exchange. She wasn't paid, but the cakes that had passed their salable prime* she got to take home and of course she shared so that we were rarely without dry but delicious cakes. Being without a job, I went on writing—books, essays, short stories. Regularly they went out and just as regularly came back. Even if they had been good, they would have come back because publishers were hardest hit of all. When people are broke,* the first things they give up are books. I couldn't even afford postage on the manuscripts. My agents,* McIntosh & Otis, paid it, although they couldn't sell my work. Needless to say, they are still my agents, and most of the work written at that time has since been published.

Given the sea and the gardens, we did pretty well with a minimum of theft. We didn't have to steal much. Farmers and orchardists* in the nearby countryside couldn't sell their crops. They gave us all the fruit and truck* we could carry home. We used to go on walking trips carrying our gunnysacks. If we had a dollar, we could buy a live sheep, for two dollars a pig, but we had to slaughter them and carry them home on our backs, or camp beside them and eat them there. We even did that.

Keeping clean was a problem because soap cost money. For a time we washed our laundry with a soap made of pork fat, wood ashes and salt. It worked, but it took a lot of sunning to get the smell out of the sheets.

For entertainment we had the public library, endless talk, long walks, any number of games. We played music, sang and made love. Enormous invention went into our pleasures. Anything at all was an excuse for a party: all holidays, birthdays called for celebration. When we felt the need to celebrate and the calendar was blank, we simply proclaimed a Jacks-Are-Wild* Day.

Now and then were came a bit of pure magic. One of us would get a small job, or a relative might go insane and enclose money in a letter—two dollars, and once or twice, God help me, five. Then word would fly through the neighborhood. Desperate* need would be taken care of first, but after that we felt desperate need for a party. Since our clothing was increasingly ratty,* it was usually a costume party. The girls wanted to look pretty, and they didn't have the clothes for it. A costume party made all manner of drapes and curtains and tablecloths available.

Hamburger was three pounds for a quarter. One third of that weight was water. I don't know how the chain stores got so much water in the meat. Of course it cooked out, but only a fool would throw the juice away. Browned flour added to it and we had delicious gravy, particularly with fresh-gathered mushrooms or the big black ones we had gathered and dried. The girls shampooed their hair with soaproot, an onion-shaped plant that grew wild; it works, too. We rarely had whisky or gin. That would have ruined the budget. There was local wine—and pretty good too; at least it didn't kill us. It was twenty cents a gallon—take your own jug. Sometimes we made it ourselves with grapes the vineyardists* let us pick. And there you had a party. Often we made them quite formal, a kind of travesty* on the kind of party we thought the rich gave. A windup phonograph furnished the music and the records were so worn down that it could be called Lo-Fi, but it was loud.

I remember one great meat loaf carried in shoulder high like a medieval boar's head at a feast. It was garnished* with strips of crisp bacon cut from an advertisement in **The Saturday Evening Post.** One day in a pile of rubbish behind Holman's store I found a papier-mâché roast turkey, the kind they put in window displays around Thanksgiving. I took it home and repaired it and gave it a new coat of paint. We used it often, served on a platter surrounded with dandelions. Under the hollow turkey was a pile of hamburgers.

It wasn't all fun and parties. When my Airedale* got sick, the veterinary said she could be cured and it would cost twenty-five dollars. We just couldn't raise it, and Tillie took about two weeks to die. If people sitting up with her and holding her head could have saved her, she would have got well. Things like that made us feel angry and helpless. But mostly we made the best of it because despondency,* not prosperity,* was just around the corner. We were more afraid of that than anything. That's why we played so hard.

JOHN STEINBECK, "A Primer on the Thirties"

*Gloss **assets**   advantages
rotated   alternated, were planted in turns
abalones   large shellfish
kelp   seaweed

sculpin kind of fish
inventiveness skill, creativeness
dough money (slang)
salable prime best time for sale
broke without money (slang)
agents business managers
orchardists owners and cultivators of fruit trees
truck vegetables
Jacks are wild Jacks (in a card game) can substitute for any other card
a Jacks-Are-Wild Day a day when any celebration can take place
desperate very great
ratty torn and old (slang)
vineyardists owners of vineyards, growers of grapes
travesty mocking imitation
garnished decorated
Airedale breed of dog
despondency hopelessness, misery
prosperity good fortune, wealth

From Steinbeck's account of his life in the 1930s during the Depression, write an account of how his life and his family's life would have been different if they had been living in different times. Discuss food, jobs, and entertainment.

Vocabulary hints If they **had** . . . , they **might have** . . .
 would have
 could have
probably; it is possible that; in all likelihood; presumably

• 5. Task (group or individual)

Rewrite the second paragraph of Steinbeck's account of the Thirties as if he were writing in the 1930s describing his **present** situation. Use the present tense.
 Begin with:

The Depression <u>is</u> no financial shock to me.

Underline all the changes you make.

• • 6. Task (group or individual)

Read the story by Ray Bradbury on p. 144. Speculate on what the world might be like in the year 2005. Write two or three paragraphs discussing what **may, might, could,** or **will** probably happen. Here are some topics you could consider: housing, food, jobs, marriage, children, education, entertainment, travel, transportation, clothes, sports, cities.

• 7. Task (individual)

Write one short paragraph beginning:

If I ever live on Mars. . . .

Then rewrite it as

If I ever lived on Mars. . . .

Look carefully at your two paragraphs. Which one indicates that you think it might be possible to live on Mars one day?

• 8. Task (group or individual)

Complete the following sentences:

a. If all prisons were abolished,
b. If parents chose their children's future marriage partners,
c. If there is a drought next summer,
d. If you worry too much,
e. If it were illegal to own a gun,
f. If people don't get married by the time they are thirty,
g. The world would be a happier place if
h. Unemployment will rise next year unless
i. Soldiers would not have deserted from the army if
j. You would have learned more if

• • 9. Task (individual)

Read the passage below and then do the task that follows.

IMPRACTICAL ADVICE TO MEET EVERY OCCASION

Never commit suicide when the water is icy. You'll merely cut yourself.

Kiss briefly, if at all. Otherwise, you might enjoy yourself.

When smiling, keep a mirror handy. It might remind you how funny things are.

If you ever get short of money, remember that life is essentially mystical.

The harder you pray, the more a mountain remains where it is.

Try to be sleeping when you dream.

When you get drunk, remember that life is short and you'll soon be sober.

Grow old, if at all, reluctantly.*

If you're young, don't brag.* You were just lucky to get off to a late start.

153

If you can't achieve sanity, then resign yourself to mere happiness.

If your arm hurts you, try to think how nice the other arm feels by comparison. If that arm also hurts, then you ought to see a doctor.

Every day, practice something.

When you get perfect, stop.

MARVIN COHEN, **Fables at Life's Expense**

*Gloss **reluctantly** unwillingly
brag boast, talk about oneself with pride

Notice that some of the sentences of advice in the passage are written as commands; others are written as conditions. Write your own list of advice to a young person. Notice the commas in those sentences beginning with **if** or **when.**

• 10. Task (group or individual)

Combine the following groups of sentences. Keep the meaning the same and write only **one** sentence for each group.

a. My father owned a cottage.
The cottage was tiny.
The cottage had three rooms.
The cottage was in Pacific Grove in California.

b. I must drop the "I" for "we" now.
There was a fairly large group of us kids.
The kids were poor.
We all lived alike.

c. Dentistry was out of the question.
My teeth went to pieces.

d. I was without a job.
I went on writing.

e. My agents paid postage.
My agents were McIntosh and Otis.
They couldn't sell my work.

f. Keeping clean was a problem.
Soap cost money.

g. We played music.
We sang.
We made love.

You can check on pp. 149–151 to see which choices Steinbeck made.

FOCUS B: RHETORICAL STRUCTURE

Do the tasks your teacher recommends.

Scientists work with hypotheses. They speculate about what will happen as a result of an action in the laboratory. Doctors make hypotheses too: they prescribe a drug or an operation, speculating that the treatment will improve the patient's condition. Hypotheses occur in writing a great deal: in advertising ("If you use this toothpaste, romance will enter your life!"), journalism, and academic writing. Writers speculate about what the world might be like in ten years' time; they speculate about the future size of the population and about the amount of food and energy resources that will be available; they speculate about what will happen to the average family if no wage increases are given this year; they speculate about what influenced a poet's work. When you write to try to persuade readers to take specific action in the future, you will usually point out what will happen if they do what you recommend and what will happen if they don't. That is speculating.

When you speculate, you have to pay special attention to the organization of your ideas. As the events have not occurred in reality, actual spatial or chronological organization is not possible. You can, therefore, work out a possible logical chronology for your hypothetical events, or you can organize the events according to importance, with the most important one last.

1. Imagine that a plan has been proposed to abolish cars from a city or town that you know well. Speculate about the effects of this change on people, business, stores, city life, entertainment, restaurants, public transportation.

2. Propose a change in a law of a country, or a rule of an institution like a school or hospital, and speculate about what the results of this change might be.

3. Write an essay of three to four paragraphs in which you speculate about how things would have been different if the South had won the Civil War, or if Man had not gone to the moon, or if . . . (choose any event in history that might have happened but did not).

4. Write an essay in which you speculate about what might happen to you and how your life would change if there were a depression like the Thirties' Depression.

5. Look at the painting **Still Life** by Fantin-Latour on p. 15. If you were going to paint a still life, what objects would you choose, and why, and how would you arrange those objects? Write two paragraphs and accompany your speculations with a sketch.

6. Speculate about some of the reasons people might possibly have for de-
ciding to:

live alone in the country
become vegetarians
give all their money to charity
join a monastic order
study medicine
drop out of school

14

ARGUING AND PERSUADING

Focus on these syntactic structures

verbs
> conditions
> modal verbs

verb phrases
> **recommend that, urge that,** etc. + (someone or something) + base form of verb
> verb (**have, make let**) + (someone) + base form of verb
> verb (**allow, tell,** etc.) + (someone) + **to** + base form of verb

modifiers: superlative forms

capitals

clauses: **because**

sentence division and punctuation: subject and predicate

sentence combining

Focus on these rhetorical structures

supporting an argument, point by point

appealing to logic or to the emotions

using varied methods to develop an argument

INTRODUCTION

Even something as simple as "I think you should buy the brown shirt" is an example of argument and persuasion. If you are then asked "Why?" you give reasons to support your argument: "It isn't as expensive as the green one. It will go well with your brown shoes. The color suits you." When you speak, you support your argument without thinking about logic and organization. When you write, you can use the same techniques that you have been using all your life, but now you have to organize your ideas and make sure they are clear and logical. Your listener can remind you about the good points of the green shirt; your reader can't, so you have to anticipate all the arguments he might raise.

CORE COMPOSITION

SCHOOL QUESTIONNAIRE

Dear Parents:

In the past, the primary purpose of our school's scholarship fund has been to racially integrate the school. To determine if the goals of this fund should remain the same, we are presenting each parent with an opportunity to express his or her view. Listed below are two statements. Please select the one which most clearly expresses your view, or express your own feelings if they are substantially different.

1. A significant number of the scholarships should be awarded to needy minority families. The remaining scholarships should be awarded on a financial-need basis to non-minority persons.

2. All scholarships should be awarded to families on the basis of their financial need, regardless of racial background.

3. Other: _____
_____

1. The questionnaire you have just read was sent by a private nursery and kindergarten school in a big city to the parents of children at the school (ages three to six). Tuition fees for one year are about $1,700 for a 9 a.m. to 3 p.m. school day. The school gives financial scholarships to about fourteen children a year; this financial aid gives partial but not full tuition assistance.

   In the questionnaire, parents are asked to express a point of view on an issue of educational, financial, and social concern to parents, children, school teachers and administrators. Discuss with other students what parents should consider before they make a decision to check number 1,

2, or 3. Discuss what other recommendations parents might make, under number 3 of the questionnaire.

2. Write a letter to two parents persuading them to check number 1, 2, or 3 on the questionnaire. State **your** point of view and present arguments for it. Use examples, division, comparison and contrast, definition, speculation, or quotation from authorities to develop and support your point of view. Imagine that your readers are totally undecided. Try to persuade them by rational, logical, and unemotional arguments. Write about four or five paragraphs.

3. Exchange letters with another student, read and discuss them, and together write answers to the following questions:

Questions How many paragraphs did you write?

Can you write one sentence that will summarize the point made in each paragraph?

Do all your points relate directly to the topic?

What methods have you used to develop your argument? Look at the chapters of this book: have you used any of those methods of development? Which ones?

Does the letter have one sentence that expresses the main idea? That is, if you had to throw away the letter and keep only one sentence to remind you of the main idea, which sentence would it be?

Could that sentence be placed anywhere else in the letter for the same or a more powerful effect?

Is your argument presented logically and unemotionally?

OCUS A: SYNTACTIC STRUCTURE

Do the tasks your teacher recommends.

• • 1. Task (individual)

Write a letter describing a problem that you have, one that you might write about to "Dear Abby," an advice column in the newspaper.

Imagine that you are now "Dear Abby." Write a reply to your letter; in one paragraph, summarize the problem

(Dear "Worried," You said that you . . .)

and in a second paragraph, suggest ways to solve the problem.

Vocabulary hints should; ought to; you had better (+ base form of verb); you might try; you must; it would be a good idea to; it is not worth -ing

(§1) • • 2. Task (group)

Exchange with another student the letter you wrote to "Dear Abby" in Task 1, above.

Imagine that you are "Dear Abby's" advisor. Write a report for "Dear Abby" telling her what you would advise the writer to do.

Vocabulary hints

I recommend } suggest } that the writer { try } go } that the writer { have } take

$\left.\begin{array}{l}\text{I recommend}\\ \text{suggest}\\ \text{propose}\\ \text{urge}\end{array}\right\}$ that the writer $\left\{\begin{array}{l}\text{try}\\ \text{go}\\ \text{have}\\ \text{take}\end{array}\right.$

It is $\left.\begin{array}{l}\text{essential}\\ \text{important}\\ \text{necessary}\\ \text{urgent}\\ \text{vital}\end{array}\right\}$ that the writer $\left\{\begin{array}{l}\text{communicate}\\ \text{experiment}\\ \text{learn}\\ \text{adjust}\\ \text{consult}\end{array}\right.$

Notice that the **base form** of the verb is used.

• • 3. Task (individual)

Write a letter to a newspaper recommending four or five changes in the town or city that you live in. Support your recommendations.

Vocabulary hints

See Task 1 and Task 2.

• 4. Task (group or individual)

A mad scientist has offered to design a computer-directed robot to help you with your everyday life. Persuade the scientist to program the robot to behave in certain ways. Make recommendations, and convince the scientist of the need for this job to be done.

Vocabulary hints

$\left.\begin{array}{l}\text{Have}\\ \text{Make}\\ \text{Let}\end{array}\right\}$ the robot **clean** my shoes every day.

The robot $\left.\begin{array}{l}\text{should}\\ \text{must}\\ \text{has to}\\ \text{ought to}\end{array}\right\}$ **clean** my shoes every day.

Teach ⎫
Tell ⎪
Allow ⎬ the robot **to clean** my shoes every day.
Get ⎪
Program ⎭

• • 5. Task (group or individual)

Reread the science fiction story by Ray Bradbury on p. 144. Imagine that it is now 2005 and you are an aggressive and ambitious travel agent devising an intensive nationwide advertising campaign to persuade people to spend their vacations on Mars. Write an advertisement that you would place in the newspapers and describe—or draw—what visual material (photographs, drawings, etc.) would accompany your copy. Use **if** clauses and superlatives in your advertisement.

Vocabulary If you go to Mars, you will . . .
hints

the most fascinating . . .
Mars is the newest . . .
the most fashionable . . .

• 6. Task (group or individual)

In the letter you wrote for the Core Composition of this chapter, did you use any words that indicate nationality? If so, did those words have capital letters: Spanish, Chinese, American, European, etc.?

Take a page from any current newspaper or magazine. Write down all the words on that page that have capital letters, other than titles or the first word in a sentence. Repeat this task with two more pages from different newspapers or magazines. Now classify all the words you have listed, for example: names of people, names of buildings, nationalities, days, months, etc.

• 7. Task (individual)

Write five statements of what **should** be done to improve the school you are attending.

To each statement, add **one** reason why you are making this recommendation. Use **because.**

Example More student advisors **should** be employed **because** many students do not know which courses to register for.

• **8.** Task (group or individual)

Combine the following groups of sentences. Keep the meaning the same and write only **one** sentence for each group.

a. The bridge is majestic.
The bridge is 746 feet high.
The bridge has 499 known victims to date.
The bridge is the No. 1 spot for death leaps in the world.

b. They have been assisted by tower television cameras.
They have been assisted by three police cars.
They have stopped 1,440 people from jumping.

c. His studies indicate (something).
Only 4% of 1,440 went on to commit suicide elsewhere.
The 1,440 were prevented from jumping.

d. They maintain (something).
Such a barrier would be ugly.
It would destroy the view.
It would be ineffective anyway.
It would only force people to go elsewhere to kill themselves.

e. You should remove the drama.
You should make bridge suicides look silly.

You can check on pp. 163–165 to see which choices one writer made.

• **9.** Task (individual)

Rewrite each of the original short sentences in Task 8 above as **yes/no** questions. Then underline the subject of each sentence.

Example Such a barrier would be ugly.
Would <u>such a barrier</u> be ugly?

FOCUS B: RHETORICAL STRUCTURE

Do the tasks your teacher recommends.

When you want to persuade your reader to accept your opinion or take action, you can use any of the methods of developing compositions that you have practiced in the earlier chapters. As part of your argument, you can describe people, places, and events, explain, divide, compare, contrast, define, speculate, and report other sources of information. This will help you to present an argument based on logic rather than emotion.

Here are some questions that might be helpful for you to ask yourself **before** you begin to write an argument:

1. Who are my readers? How much do they know about this topic?

2. What do I want my readers to **do** as a result of my argument? (Accept it, just think about it, or act on it?)

3. Which **one** sentence will sum up my argument? Where will I place such a sentence in my essay?

4. How many points will I make in support of my argument, and what are they?

5. How will I develop each one? Can, and should, any points be defined, divided, supported with examples, or compared?

6. Have I done all my research on the topic? Do I know what other people say about it? Which authorities should I quote or paraphrase to support my own argument? Which opposing views should I refute?

7. Does my topic contain any terms that are complicated enough to need an extended definition? Where will I put my definition?

8. In what order will I organize my points? Which one should be first? last?

9. Do I believe what I am saying?

1. Read the following article about the Golden Gate Bridge and the proposal for a suicide prevention barrier. Summarize in your own words the situation, the two opposing views, the reasons people give for holding those views, and write a statement of **your** views and your reasons for holding these views. Imagine that you are writing to try to influence members of the board of directors to vote for or against the plan.

RIGHT TO LEAP OFF GOLDEN GATE AT ISSUE ON COAST

San Francisco.
The thought of that dizzying, breath-stopping, last look downward before stepping off into space from the Golden Gate Bridge has long held a powerful fascination for San Franciscans.

This is the nation's premier suicide* city—one of every 2,300 San Franciscans kills himself here every year—and the majestic, 746-foot-high Bridge, with 499 known victims to date, is the No. 1 spot for death leaps in the world.

But this fall the question of suicide, or more specifically the right of an individual to commit it if he wants to, has acquired a rare topicality* and more than a touch of controversy.*

This is because for the first time in the 36-year history of the Bridge, the independent* board of directors that controls its operations has announced tentative* plans to erect a $1-million suicide prevention barrier.

The proposed barrier is now undergoing wind velocity* tests in

Washington. If a majority of the 18-member board of directors votes in favor of the plan at a meeting next winter, the eight-foot-high iron fence could be installed in place of the current three-and-a-half-foot one early next year.

1,440 Leaps Averted*

So far responsibility for preventing suicides has rested with the 98-man force that operates the bridge. Assisted by tower television cameras that scan pedestrians and three police cars, they have stopped 1,440 people from jumping in the last ten years.

But the possibility that the public's freedom to jump off the bridge might be revoked* has turned the matter into a battle between "humanitarians," who oppose that freedom, and "civil libertarians," who affirm* it.

And as this was taking place, the 497th, 498th and 499th persons jumped off the Bridge and now the city is waiting daily for the 500th.

"The whole thing is like Hank Aaron's home run,"* said Herb Caen, a local columnist who supports the barrier even though his newspaper, **The San Francisco Chronicle,** does not.

So intense is interest in No. 500 that for several days the city's television stations positioned camera crews on the bridge in a 'round-the-clock wait.

On the question whether to install the barrier the local news media have vigorously* lined up on both sides.

Supporters of the proposal include most well-known politicians, especially those who are up for re-election,* medical associations and religious groups.

They maintain, as City Supervisor Peter Tamares put it: "Even if we save one life, it's worth the cost."

According to Dr. Richard Seiden, a psychologist at the University of California's School of Public Health at Berkeley who has studied the situation for several years, the Bridge has some kind of "mystical attraction" for the anguished and depressed.

This lure,* he says, is so powerful that it leads people to commit suicide who would otherwise survive their bouts of depression.

His studies indicate, he adds, that only 4 per cent of the 1,440 who were prevented from jumping went on to commit suicide elsewhere.

Opponents of the barrier include about 75 percent of the people who have written the Bridge authority on the issue and many of the local artists, writers and architects as well as some of San Francisco's best-known citizens.

They maintain that such a barrier would be ugly, would destroy the view, and would be ineffective anyway since it would only force people to go elsewhere to kill themselves. But they also tend to feel strongly about the right to kill oneself. "I think," Kurt Adler, the opera director, said in an interview, "it is everyone's privilege to decide if he wants to live or not. It is not for society to decide that."

And one woman who wrote in from Maine suggested: "You should try a little reverse psychology and put up a diving board at a strategic point, with a hook for hanging your jacket and some paper and even a mail box for suicide notes. You should remove the drama and make bridge suicides look silly."

LACEY FOSBURGH, **The New York Times,** October 5, 1973

°**Gloss** **suicide** killing oneself
acquired a rare topicality become news for a change
controversy argument
independent self-governing
tentative experimental
velocity speed
averted prevented
revoked taken away
affirm support
Hank Aaron's home run the baseball player's home run (hit over the fence) that broke the record
vigorously energetically
up for re-election running for political office, hoping to be elected again
lure attraction
bouts periods

2. Read the essay by Steinbeck about the Depression of the 1930's on p. 149. Imagine that you are in a similar situation—living in a Depression with no job, very little money, and very little food. You hear of a job that you would like. Write a letter to the employer, trying to persuade him to accept you for the job. He will probably receive hundreds of letters, so you have to convince him that you are the best candidate. Give **logical** reasons why he should choose you: refer to your experience, qualifications, character, integrity, etc., with examples.

   Now write another letter to the same employer, also trying to persuade him to accept you for the job. This time, appeal to his emotions, instead of to his logic. Tell him how you need the job, tell him about your poverty, your living conditions, your family, your health, your personal circumstances. Give examples that will make him feel sorry for you.

   Read both letters. If you were the employer, which type of letter would you find more persuasive? Why?

   Exchange letters with another student. Read the two letters and write an employer's reply to one of them.

3. Think of a way in which an institution—a school, a hospital, a business,

etc.—could and should be changed. Write a letter to the President of the institution, and argue for this change. Give reasons why it is necessary and recommend how the change should be made. What will be the effects of the change?

4. Look again at the painting **Nighthawks** by Edward Hopper on p. 32. Imagine that you are a frequent customer at the coffee shop. Some people in the town do not like the fact that the coffee shop stays open until late at night; they have written a letter to the local newspaper demanding that it be closed. Write a letter in reply, summarizing their position and their reasons and giving your reasons for keeping it open. Remember to give logical reasons that might persuade your opponents. Add a final paragraph in which you make an emotional argument.

5. A friend of yours is having some emotional difficulties that affect work, family, personal relationships. The friend does not have much money, but is considering consulting a psychiatrist on a weekly basis. Give advice as to whether he should or should not do this and give reasons. Explain to your friend what the alternatives are.

6. You are a real estate agent trying to persuade people to rent the apartment illustrated below. Write persuasive letters to (a) a single man with a well-paid job, (b) a divorced woman with three small children, and (c) three student nurses, telling them the advantages of the apartment for their own particular situation.

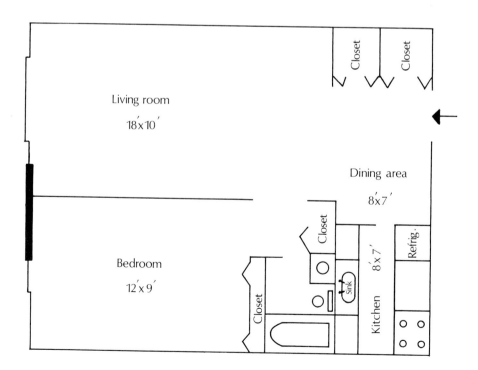

7. You have received an application for the apartment from a single woman who plays the French horn in her spare time. This would probably make all the other tenants angry. Write a letter to her, without mentioning the French horn, and try to dissuade her from taking the apartment. This time you will point out all its disadvantages.

8. Read three editorials in newspapers. Clip them out and write a few sentences for each summarizing the point the writer is making. Choose **one** of the editorials and write your own newspaper editorial in reply, taking the opposite point of view.

9. Look at advertisements for cars in newspapers and magazines. Write an advertisement for a new car. Praise all its latest innovations and try to make your advertisement appeal to a particular group of people: the young, the sporty, housewives, families, or the wealthy, for example.

10. With another student, pretend that one of you is a volunteer working for a HELP telephone line, who listens to people's problems and offers advice. Pretend the other one of you calls in with a terrible problem of health, family, or money, and threatens to do something drastic about it. One student writes the problem, with as many details as possible to help the advisor. The other student writes the reply, giving advice and trying to persuade the caller not to carry out the threat.

APPENDIX

Complete versions of reading passages used in the text

SHERWOOD ANDERSON
WINESBURG, OHIO

Doctor Parcival **was** a large man with a drooping mouth covered by a yellow mustache. He always **wore** a dirty white waistcoat out of the pockets of which protruded a number of the kind of black cigars known as stogies. His teeth **were** black and irregular and there **was** something strange about his eyes. The lid of the left eye **twitched**; it **fell** down and **snapped** up; it **was** exactly as though the lid of the eye were a window shade and someone stood inside the doctor's head playing with the cord.

(Chapter 2, p. 23.)

OSCAR LEWIS
LIFE IN A MEXICAN VILLAGE

The qualities looked for in a spouse vary considerably between boys and girls. In selecting a wife, boys generally choose a girl for romantic reasons, beauty, or personality. Girls tend to be more realistic about selecting a husband and will often refuse to marry a boy who is known to drink, chase women, be violent, or be lazy. However, status factors are very important in marriage. It is usual for boys to seek out a girl who is poorer and who has the same or less education, so that "the man can be the boss" and his family need not be ashamed before her. Tepoztecan boys tend to "respect" and avoid having affairs with girls from the more important and prosperous families, for fear of incurring reprisals from the parents of such girls. Girls, on the other hand, seek to improve their economic status with marriage, and it is rare for a girl to marry a man with less education. As a result of these attitudes, the daughters of the families in the upper economic group in the village have difficulty finding husbands. They tend to marry later, and to marry more educated men or men from the outside. Occasionally a wealthy girl in her late twenties will marry a boy poorer than herself rather than remain unmarried.

(Chapter 4, p. 49.)

GEORGE PLIMPTON
"HEMINGWAY," THE PARIS REVIEW INTERVIEWS

A working habit he has had from the beginning, Hemingway stands when he writes. He stands in a pair of his oversized loafers on the worn skin of a Lesser Kudu—the typewriter and the reading board chest-high opposite him.

When Hemingway starts on a project he always begins with a pencil, using the reading board to write on onionskin typewriter paper. He keeps a sheaf of the blank paper on a clipboard to the left of the typewriter, extracting the paper a sheet at a time from under a metal clip which reads "These Must Be Paid." He places the paper slantwise on the reading board, leans against the board with his left arm, steadying the paper with his hand, and fills the paper with handwriting which through the years has become larger, more boyish, with a paucity of punctuation, very few capitals, and often the period marked with an x. The page completed, he clips it face-down on another clipboard which he places off to the right of the typewriter.

Hemingway shifts to the typewriter, lifting off the reading board, only when the writing is going fast and well, or when the writing is, for him at least, simple: dialogue, for instance.

He keeps track of his daily progress—"so as not to kid myself"—on a large chart made out of the side of a cardboard packing-case and set up against the wall under the nose of a mounted gazelle head. The numbers on the chart showing the daily output of words differ from 450, 575, 462, 1250, back to 512, the higher figures on days Hemingway puts in extra work so he won't feel guilty spending the following day fishing on the Gulf Stream.

(Chapter 4, p. 50.)

DASHIELL HAMMETT
THE MALTESE FALCON

Fill in the numbered blanks with words that could fit the meaning, tone, and grammar of the passage. The author's words appear upside-down at the end of the passage. Do not look at them until after you have made your choice.

A telephone bell rang in darkness. When it had rung three times bed-springs creaked, fingers fumbled on wood, something small and hard thudded* on a carpeted floor, the springs creaked again, and a man's voice said: "Hello. . . . Yes, speaking. . . . Dead? . . . Yes. . . . Fifteen minutes. Thanks."

A switch clicked and a (1)_____ bowl hung on three (2)_____ chains from the ceiling's center filled the room with light. Spade, barefooted in green and white (3)_____ pajamas, sat on the side of his bed. He scowled at the telephone on the table while his hands took from beside it a packet of brown paper and a sack of Bull Durham.* Cold (4)_____ air blew in through two open windows, bringing with it half a dozen times a minute the Alcatraz* foghorn's (5)_____ moaning. A (6)_____ alarm-clock, (7)_____ mounted on a corner of Duke's **Celebrated Criminal Cases of America**—face down on the table—held its hands at five minutes past two.

Spade's (8)_____ fingers made a cigarette with (9)_____ care, sifting a measured quantity of tan flakes down into curved paper, spreading the flakes so that they lay equal at the ends with a slight depression in the middle, thumbs rolling the paper's inner edge down and up under the outer edge as forefingers pressed it over, thumbs and fingers sliding to the paper cylinder's ends to hold it even while tongue licked the flap, left forefinger and thumb pinching their end while right forefinger and thumb smoothed the (10)_____ seam, right forefinger and thumb twisting their end and lifting the other to Spade's mouth. He picked up the (11)_____ and nickel lighter that had fallen to the floor, manipulated it, and with the cigarette burning in a corner of his mouth stood up. He took off his pajamas. The (12)_____ thickness of his arms, legs, and body, the sag* of his big (13)_____ shoulders, made his body like a bear's. It was like a shaved bear's: his chest was hairless. His skin was (14)_____ soft and pink.

He scratched the back of his neck and began to dress. He put on a thin white union-suit, (15)_____ socks, black garters, and (16)_____ brown shoes. When he had fastened his shoes he picked up the telephone, called Graystone 4500, and ordered a taxicab. He put on a green-striped white shirt, a (7)_____ white collar, a green necktie, the gray suit he had worn that day, a loose tweed overcoat, and a dark gray hat. The street-door-bell rang as he stuffed tobacco, keys, and money into his pockets.

(Chapter 5, p. 58.)

*Gloss **thudded** dropped with a dull sound
Bull Durham brand of tobacco
Alcatraz prison on island in San Francisco Bay
sag droop, hanging

1. white 2. gilded (= painted gold) 3. checked 4. steamy
5. dull 6. tinny 7. insecurely 8. thick 9. deliberate
10. damp 11. pigskin 12. smooth 13. rounded
14. childishly 15. gray 16. dark 17. soft

JOAN DIDION
PLAY IT AS IT LAYS

She had watched them in supermarkets and she knew the signs. At seven o'clock on a Saturday evening they would be standing in the checkout line reading the horoscope in **Harper's Bazaar** and in their carts would be a single lamb chop and maybe two cans of cat food and the Sunday morning paper, the early edition with the comics wrapped outside. They would be very pretty some of the time, their skirts the right length and their sunglasses the right tint and maybe only a little vulnerable tightness around the mouth, but there they were, one lamb chop and some cat food and the morning paper. To avoid giving off the signs, Maria shopped always for a household, gallons of grapefruit juice, quarts of green chile salsa, dried lentils and alphabet noodles, rigatoni and canned yams, twenty-pound boxes of laundry detergent. She knew all the indices to the idle lonely, never bought a small tube of toothpaste, never dropped a magazine in her shopping cart. The house in Beverly Hills overflowed with sugar, corn-muffin mix, frozen roasts and Spanish onions. Maria ate cottage cheese.

(Chapter 5, p. 63.)

JOHN STEINBECK
TRAVELS WITH CHARLEY

Not far outside of Bangor I stopped at an auto court* and rented a room. It wasn't expensive. The sign said "Greatly Reduced Winter Rates." It was immaculate;* everything was done in plastics—the floors, the curtain, table tops of stainless burnless plastic, lamp shades of plastic. Only the bedding and the towels were of a natural material. I went to the small restaurant run in conjunction.* It was all plastic too—the table linen, the butter dish. The sugar and crackers were wrapped in cellophane,* the jelly in a small plastic coffin sealed with cellophane. It was early evening and I was the only customer. Even the waitress wore a sponge-off apron. . . .

I went back to my clean little room. I don't ever drink alone. It's not much fun. And I don't think I will until I am an alcoholic. But this night I got a bottle of vodka from my stores and took it to my cell. In the bathroom two water tumblers* were sealed in cellophane sacks with the words: "These glasses are sterilized* for your protection." Across the toilet seat a strip of paper bore* the message: "This seat has been sterilized with ultraviolet light for your protection." Everyone was protecting me and it was horrible. I tore the glasses from their covers. I violated the toilet-seat seal with my foot. I poured half a tumbler of vodka and drank it and then another. Then I lay deep in hot water in the tub and I was utterly miserable, and nothing was good anywhere.

(Chapter 5, p. 67.)

*Gloss   **auto court**   motel
        immaculate   spotless, very clean
        in conjunction   along with (the motel)
        cellophane   thin, transparent paper for wrapping
        sterilized   made pure and sanitary
        tumblers   glasses
        bore   carried

RICHARD BRAUTIGAN
"ONE AFTERNOON IN 1939"

This is a constant story that I keep telling my daughter who is four years old. She gets something from it and wants to hear it again and again.

When it's time for her to go to bed, she says, "Daddy, tell me about when you were a kid and climbed inside that rock."

"OK."

She cuddles the covers about her as if they were controllable clouds and puts her thumb in her mouth and looks at me with listening blue eyes.

"Once when I was a little kid, just your age, my mother and father took me on a picnic to Mount Rainier. We drove up there in an old car and saw a deer standing in the middle of the road.

"We came to a meadow where there was snow in the shadows of the trees and snow in the places where the sun didn't shine.

"There were wild flowers growing in the meadow and they looked beautiful. In the middle of the meadow there was a huge round rock and Daddy walked over to the rock and found a hole in the center of it and looked inside. The rock was hollow like a small room.

"Daddy crawled inside the rock and sat there staring out at the blue sky and the wild flowers. Daddy really liked that rock and pretended that it was a house and he played inside the rock all afternoon.

"He got some smaller rocks and took them inside the big rock. He pretended that the smaller rocks were a stove and furniture and things and he cooked a meal, using wild flowers for food."

That's the end of the story.

Then she looks up at me with her deep blue eyes and sees me as a child playing inside a rock, pretending that wild flowers are hamburgers and cooking them on a small stove-like rock.

She can never get enough of this story. She has heard it thirty or forty times and always wants to hear it again.

It's very important to her.

I think she uses this story as a kind of Christopher Columbus door to the discovery of her father when he was a child and her contemporary.

(Chapter 6, p. 70.)

JAMES THURBER
"THE CASE AGAINST WOMEN"

Another reason I hate women (and I am speaking, I believe, for the American male generally) is that in almost every case where there is a sign reading "Please have exact change ready," a woman never has anything smaller than a ten-dollar bill. She gives ten-dollar bills to bus conductors and change men in subways and other such persons who deal in nickels and dimes and quarters. Recently, in Bermuda, I saw a woman hand the conductor on the little railway there a bill of such huge denomination that I was utterly unfamiliar with it. I was sitting too far away to see exactly what it was, but I had the feeling that it was a five-hundred-dollar bill. The conductor merely ignored it and stood there waiting—the fare was just one shilling. Eventually, scrabbling* around in her handbag, the woman found a shilling. All the men on the train who witnessed the transaction tightened up inside; that's what a woman with a ten-dollar bill or a twenty or a five-hundred does to a man in such situations—she tightens him up inside. The episode gives him the feeling that some monstrous triviality* is threatening the whole structure of civilization. It is difficult to analyze this feeling, but there it is.

(Chapter 6, p. 75.)

*Gloss scrabbling   scratching, searching
        monstrous triviality   a small thing, appearing terrible (and terribly large)

HENRY DAVID THOREAU
WALDEN

When I first took up my abode in the woods, that is, began to spend my nights as well as days there, which, by accident, was on Independence day, or the fourth of July, 1845, my house was not finished for winter, but was merely a defence against the rain, without plastering or chimney, the walls being of rough weather-stained boards, with wide chinks, which made it cool at night.

ERNEST HEMINGWAY
"SOLDIER'S HOME"

That was the thing about French girls and German girls. There was not all this talking. You couldn't talk much and you did not need to talk. It was simple and you were friends. He thought about France and then he began to think about Germany. On the whole he had liked Germany better. He did not want to leave Germany. He did not want to come home. Still, he had come home. He sat on the front porch.

(Chapter 6, p. 76.)

The first two sentences of the paragraph by Jack Agueros are:

Junior high school was a waste. I can say with 90% accuracy that I learned nothing.

(Chapter 7, p. 82.)

H. L. MENCKEN
"TAKING STOCK"

All in all, a harsh and forbidding life, and yet, after eight and a third years, I still pursue it, and if all goes well I hope to print my thousandth article in February, 1991. In those eight and a third years I have served under four editors, not including myself; I have grown two beards and shaved them off; I have eaten 3,086 meals; I have made more than $100,000 in wages, fees, refreshers, tips and bribes; I have written 510,000 words about books and not about books; I have received, looked at, and thrown away nearly 3,000 novels; I have been called a fraud 700 times, and blushed at the proofs; I have had more than 200 invitations to lecture before women's clubs, Chautauquas, Y.M.C.A.'s, chambers of commerce, Christian Endeavor societies, and lodges of the Elks; I have received 150 pounds of letters of sweet flattery; I have myself written and published eight books, and reviewed them all favorably; I have had seventeen proposals of marriage from lady poets; I have been indicted by grand juries eight times; I have discovered thirty bogus geniuses; I have been abroad three and a half times, and learned and forgotten six foreign languages; I have attended 62 weddings, and spent nearly $200 for wedding presents; I have gained 48 pounds in weight and lost 18 pounds, and have grown bald and gray; I have been converted by the Rev. Dr. Billy Sunday, and then recanted and gone back to the devil; I have worn out nine suits of clothes; I have narrowly escaped marriage four times; I have had lumbago and neuralgia; I have taken to horn-rimmed spectacles; I have eluded the white-slave traders; I have fallen downstairs twice; I have undergone nine surgical operations; I have read the **Police Gazette** in the barbershop every week; I have shaken hands with Dr. Wilson; I have upheld the banner of the ideal; I have kept the faith, in so far as I could make out what it was; I have loved and lied; I have got old and sentimental; I have been torpedoed without warning.

(Chapter 8, p. 96.)

DAVID C. GLASS
"STRESS, COMPETITION AND HEART ATTACKS"

Most [researchers] have settled on stress and what they call "Type-A" behavior as the prime candidates for psychological causes of heart attacks. A person who shows Type-A behavior is highly competitive, feels pressured for time, and reacts to frustration with hostility. My research focuses on the interplay between the Type-A personality, life stress, and heart attack.

In order to classify people as Type A or Type B, I use their responses to questions about their ambitions, competitiveness, sense of being pressed for time, and hostile feelings. Type-A people, for example, are likely to set deadlines or quotas for themselves at work or at home at least once per week, while Type-B people do so only occasionally. A Type-A person brings his work home with him frequently, a Type-B almost never. The Type-A person is highly achievement-oriented and pushes himself to near capacity, while the Type-B person takes it easy. Hard-driving Type-A students earn more academic honors than their Type-B counterparts, though they are no more intelligent. The Type-A behavior pattern earns a person the rewards he seeks, but at a cost to his body that may be the death of him. Obviously, not all Type-A people have heart attacks, but there are certain times, especially when they come under severe stress, when their risk of heart attack is greatest.

(Chapter 9, p. 109.)

MARGARET MEAD
"ON FRIENDSHIP"

August, 1966

Few Americans stay put for a lifetime. We move from town to city to suburb, from high school to college in a different state, from a job in one region to a better job elsewhere, from the home where we raise our children to the home where we plan to live in retirement. With each move we are forever making new friends, who become part of our new life at that time.

For many of us the summer is a special time for forming new friendships. Today millions of Americans vacation abroad, and they go not only to see new sights but also—in those places where they do not feel too strange—with the hope of meeting new people. No one really expects a vacation trip to produce a close friend. But surely the beginning of a friendship is possible? Surely in every country people value friendship?

They do. The difficulty when strangers from two countries meet is not a lack of appreciation of friendship, but different expectations about what constitutes* friendship and how it comes into being. In those European countries that Americans are most likely to visit, friendship is quite sharply distinguished from other, more casual relations, and is differently related to family life. For a Frenchman, a German or an Englishman friendship is usually more particularlized* and carries a heavier burden* of commitment.*

But as we use the word, "friend" can be applied to a wide range of relationships—to someone one has known for a few weeks in a new place, to a close business associate, to a childhood playmate, to a man or woman, to a trusted confidant. There are real differences among these relations for Americans—a friendship may be superficial,* casual, situational or deep and enduring. But to a European, who sees only our surface behavior, the differences are not clear.

(Chapter 11, p. 133.)

*Gloss **constitutes** forms, creates
particularized made specific
burden duty, responsibility
commitment obligation
superficial shallow, not deep

INDEX OF SYNTACTIC STRUCTURES

References are to the page number in bold type, followed by the number of the task(s) on that page.

INDEX OF SYNTACTIC STRUCTURES

Permission to reprint copyright material is hereby gratefully acknowledged: